PARTICULAR REDEMPTION

PARTICULAR REDEMPTION

*The End and Design
of the Death of Christ*

Addresses from

A Defence of Some Important Doctrines of the Gospel:

Preached at the Lime Street Lecture

John Hurrion

*With an Introduction by Iain H. Murray
and a Preface by John Elias*

THE BANNER OF TRUTH TRUST

THE BANNER OF TRUTH TRUST
3 Murrayfield Road, Edinburgh EH12 6EL, UK
PO Box 621, Carlisle, PA 17013, USA

*

Reproduced from
A Defence of Some Important Doctrines of the Gospel:
in Twenty-six Sermons; Preached at the Lime-Street Lecture.
By Several Eminent Ministers
(8th edition; London: Richard Baynes, 1824)

*

ISBN
Print: 978 1 84871 752 7
EPUB: 978 1 84871 753 4
Kindle: 978 1 84871 754 1

*

Typeset in 11/15 pt Adobe Garamond Pro at
The Banner of Truth Trust

Printed in the USA by
Versa Press, Inc.,
East Peoria, IL.

With thankfulness for the ministry of

The Evangelical Library,

5/6 Gateway Mews, Ringway, Bounds Green,

London, N11 2UT,

an institution which has inspired many

by calling attention to the riches of the past.

Contents

Contents

Introduction

JOHN HURRION was born in Suffolk, *circa* 1675, in a period when those who had stood apart from the Church of England after the Act of Uniformity of 1662 were undergoing persecution. Almost the only knowledge we have of his youth is this statement: 'In his younger years, he was brought to a saving knowledge of Jesus Christ.'[1] In this his maternal grandfather, Edmund Whincop (1616–87), may well have played a part. After being silenced at Layston in 1662, Whincop's troubles included a five-month imprisonment, before he was called to serve a Nonconformist congregation at Watesfield in 1677. His grandson was only twelve when he died, but the fact that John Hurrion was to marry Jane Baker, daughter of a family of the Watesfield church, indicates an ongoing connexion with that congregation. The marriage took place in 1696, soon after Hurrion's settlement in a church at Denton, Norfolk, where his predecessor, William Bidbank, had served since 1662.

---

[1] W. Wilson, *History and Antiquities of Dissenting Churches and Meeting Houses in London* (London: 1810), III:288. All our information on Hurrion comes from this source, or from Abraham Taylor in *A Defence of Some Important Doctrines of the Gospel: Preached at the Lime Street Lecture* (London: Baynes, 1824).

That Hurrion was set apart for the gospel ministry about the age of twenty-one, confirms a tradition of his early studiousness. Under what conditions his training for the ministry had proceeded are not recorded, save that it was 'partly under Mr Robinson of Walpole, Suffolk'. That he was committed to hard study is certain, and his library was by no means confined to the Puritan period. We are told that one of the authors whom he held in 'particular esteem' was Chrysostom of Constantinople. He was to become, in the opinion of his friend and contemporary, Abraham Taylor, 'As judicious and accomplished a Divine as any that appeared in his age.' That this was not study for study's sake is clear from the influence of his ministry at Denton. From a weak condition at the time of his settlement, the work 'by the blessing of God upon his labours was brought into a very flourishing state. His great abilities gained him also a large share in the affections and esteem of several other churches in that and the neighbouring counties.'

By the 1690s, evangelical churches in the Nonconformist tradition were facing new dangers. While 'the Glorious Revolution' of 1688 had ended physical persecution, the Nonconformist churches (termed 'Dissenters' by members of the Church of England) were beginning to form denominations, only to have their unity threatened from another direction as the former biblical orthodoxy came to be challenged. In Suffolk the rise of anti-trinitarian belief had an advocate in William Manning, said to have influenced the

Presbyterian, Thomas Emlyn, who became, possibly, the first Nonconformist to declare himself a Unitarian. At some point after Hurrion's settlement at Denton, Manning made strong attempts to win him over, thinking 'he would be a considerable gain to his party'. His endeavours had the opposite effect. After giving much attention to the subject, Hurrion's whole ministry was to be characterized by emphasis on the deity of Christ and the Holy Spirit. It was his later counsel that, 'whether the Trinity was opposed or no, young divines could not take a better way to fit themselves for public service, than to be rooted and grounded in that important doctrine'.

In the 1690s, anti-trinitarian belief had no spokesmen among the Nonconformist churches in London. That development was to await the next century, but the unity of these churches was already disrupted in that decade by a different deviation, more evangelical in its form, and strengthened by the advocacy of Richard Baxter. A general esteem for Baxter was based on the value of his well-known practical writing, most notably, *The Saints' Everlasting Rest* (1649) and *The Reformed Pastor* (1656). But in his understanding of redemption Baxter also wrote titles which departed significantly from the understanding of redemption as contained in the Westminster, Savoy and Baptist Confessions.[2] His position (largely derived from Amyraut and other writers) is succinctly stated by Isaac Ambrose in the words, 'Christ died not to

---

[2] See J. I. Packer, *Redemption & Restoration of Man in the Thought of Richard Baxter* (Vancouver: Regent College, 2003).

bring all or any man actually to salvation, but to purchase salvability and reconciliation so far, as that God might and would (*salva justitia*) deal with them on terms of a better covenant.'[3] The one 'condition' now to be fulfilled was 'faith'. The 'new covenant', Baxter wrote, 'is a general gift or act of oblivion, or pardon, given freely to all mankind, on condition they will believe and consent to it'.[4]

Christ's work of redemption, Baxter taught, is 'the beginning of your justification'. So God 'requireth no actual obedience, as the condition of our begun justification', that being done already for all people. But for justification in its entirety, he 'doth require both the continuance of faith, and actual sincere obedience, as the condition of continuing, or not losing, our justification'.[5]

In opposition to this belief, he names as '*error*' the statement: 'Christ did both perfectly obey, and also make satisfaction for sin by suffering, in the person of all the elect … so that his righteousness of obedience … is so imputed to us, as if we ourselves had done it, and suffered it … .'[6]

Baxter wrote on this teaching at various points in his life but dispute came to a head around the time of his death in London in 1691. At this date the Nonconformist leaders in London—both those of Presbyterian and those of Congregational persuasion—had been drawing together

---

[3] *Looking unto Jesus*, in *Complete Works of Isaac Ambrose* (London, 1674), p. 395.
[4] *The Life of Faith*, in *Practical Works of Richard Baxter* (London, 1830), XII:299.
[5] *Ibid.*, p. 306.
[6] *Ibid.*, p. 312.

in a Plan of Union, and were sharing in speaking at the Pinners' Hall lectures, an institution established by Puritan merchants in 1672. But as Baxter's teaching resurfaced, serious controversy ensued which ended the Union and the presence of Presbyterians at Pinners' Hall. Sympathy for an allowance of Baxter's views was chiefly, but not entirely, among Presbyterians, while Congregationalists wrote in opposition. Criticism centred on two points: (1) This was a view of justification which saw it no longer as 'an act of God's free grace' (*Shorter Catechism)* but as a process in which faith was to be regarded as a continuing element. (2) Baxter's teaching on justification resulted from a different understanding of the atonement. The confessional belief was that Christ, for those with whom he was united by the Father's gift, rendered obedience and suffered condemnation *in their place.* Those whose sin was imputed to Christ, are the same persons to whom his righteousness is imputed (Rom. 4:25; 5:10). Baxter denied, as in the words above, any such correlation.

Opponents of the new teaching in the 1690s were apprehensive that its influence would be extensive, and the first thirty years of the eighteenth century justified their concern. In Scotland, a growing number of men, who followed Baxter, got the name of 'Neonomians' ('new-law' keepers). In the words of John Macleod, 'The righteousness of God which is by faith of Jesus Christ was set aside as the ground of acceptance; and our new life as believers and penitents was looked upon as so much of the ground on which our acceptance is built.'[7] In Wales there was no such early acceptance. Howell Harris wrote: 'I think we all agree with the good old Reformers and Puritans; I hold their works in great esteem. We do not think the Baxterian scheme orthodox.'[8]

By contrast, in England the idea that Christ's death did not secure the justification of all for whom he suffered gained widespread popularity, coalescing with Arminian belief. The contemporary rise of anti-trinitarian belief, and growing rejection of Scripture as divine revelation, meant that a general decline of evangelical belief was in progress when Hurrion's material, reprinted in these pages, was published in 1732. It constituted four chapters in a larger volume, *A Defence of Some Important Doctrines of the Gospel: Preached at the Lime Street Lecture.* In a Preface it was said,

> As error never raged with greater violence than it does in our unhappy times, and as lukewarmness never discovered itself more than in the present day of darkness, it never could be more expedient than now to plead for the glorious gospel of the blessed God.[9]

There is only a minimum of information on Hurrion's life between his settlement in Norfolk in 1696 and his writing of these pages. His ministry at Denton continued through twenty-eight years, reported as 'very successful, and he was

[7] *Scottish Theology in Relation to Church History since the Reformation* (Edinburgh: Banner of Truth Trust, 1974), p. 134 (p. 139, 2015 ed.). Further on Baxter, see pp. 136-37 (pp. 141-42, 2015 ed.).

[8] Edward Morgan, *Life and Times of Howell Harris* (Holywell, 1852), p. 139.

[9] *Important Doctrines of the Gospel* (repr., 1824), p. vii.

esteemed a great blessing by all the Dissenters, in those parts'. In 1724 he was faced with the difficult decision of a call to the church at Hare Court, Aldersgate Street, London. He considered the prospect of wider usefulness, and he had concern lest declining the call would result in a division of the congregation.[10] On the other hand, he had no prevailing desire to remove. The call was accepted but the outcome was not altogether happy. Perhaps a division in the congregation existed and continued. A 'coolness' of some towards him, contrasted with his previous popularity, and a decline in his health hindered his activity in pastoral visiting.

On the wider scene, Hurrion's ability was recognized by his appointment as one of the lecturers at Pinners' Hall where he preached for the first time on June 11, 1726. Sixteen sermons which he preached there, on *The Proper Divinity and Extraordinary Works of the Holy Spirit,* were published posthumously in 1734. In 1730 London merchants, concerned over the general situation, initiated another lecture series and Hurrion was one of the eight ministers chosen to take part. Convened at Lime Street, London, these lectures started on November 12, 1730, and continued weekly to April 8, 1731. The subject assigned to him was 'The Scripture Doctrine of

---

[10] The previous, popular minister, John Nesbitt (1661–1727) had laid down the charge on account of ill-health. He was a man of the same judgment as Hurrion: 'In the close of the seventeenth century, when the controversy relating to the doctrine of justification ran high, he stood by the ancient faith, and appeared with boldness against innovations' (Wilson, *Dissenting Churches*, p. 285). Nesbitt's assistant, however, was of a more compromising spirit, and as he was to continue as an assistant, there was potential for the development of two parties in the church.

Particular Redemption', on which he was due to speak on four occasions. Ill health, however, prevented him from speaking again after he had preached twice. A publication of the Lime Street lectures was being prepared by Abraham Taylor and Hurrion endeavoured to help him. On December 14, 1731, his health seriously failing, he wrote to Taylor: 'I have now finished, and now send you, my third sermon: I shall go on with the fourth as fast as I can; if possible, I would finish it next week, but I fear I shall not be able, I have been so much worse since I wrote you last.'

Hurrion's anticipation was correct, he got no further than leaving notes of the fourth sermon, on which, Taylor said, 'I have not made any alterations.' But he must have augmented them for publication. It tells us much of the man that, at the very end of life, he gave his last energies to a subject on which he felt deeply. 'The delight he took in his subject', Taylor commented, 'carried him above his great pain and weakness.' He was 'an eminent saint', and, in dying, confessed: 'The death of Christ being the fountain of our life, there is nothing more necessary, pleasant, or useful to the Christian, than a right apprehension and remembrance of it.' John Hurrion died on December 31, 1731, in his fifty-sixth year.

The whole of the lectures as published were orientated towards the need for reformation and revival in the churches. Unknown to the authors in 1732—the year their volume was published—an instrument was in preparation by whom the doctrine Hurrion defended would spring into greater public attention. George Whitefield matriculated at Pembroke College, Oxford, in November 1732. About three years later, he wrote: 'God was pleased to enlighten, and bring me into the knowledge of his free grace, and the necessity of being justified in his sight by *faith alone.*' He was on a course which would lead him to challenge his friend, John Wesley, with the question, 'How can all be universally redeemed if all are not finally saved? You plainly make salvation depend not on God's *free grace*, but on man's *free will.*'[11]

It is remarkable that the re-emergence of Puritan belief came within the Church of England where the authors of that school had been so long discredited. Whitefield openly owned their writings. William Grimshaw came to the doctrine of justification through the reading of John Owen, and James Hervey, disagreeing with John Wesley on that doctrine, drew attention to the *Important Doctrines of the Gospel: Preached at the Lime Street Lecture,* 1732, which, he says, on final perseverance and the imputed righteousness of Christ, gave him the 'fullest view which I ever remember to have met with in any of our English writers'.[12] Hervey was not to be the last to draw attention to the influence of the 1732 volume which was in its eighth edition by 1824. In its main lines, Wesley's thinking was close to Baxter's, and when Baxter's teaching on

[11] 'A Letter to John Wesley', 1741, in *George Whitefield's Journals* (Edinburgh: Banner of Truth Trust, 1985), p. 587.

[12] For Hervey's critique of Wesley's opposition to imputed righteousness, see *Eleven Letters from the Rev. Mr Hervey to the Rev. Mr John Wesley* (London: 3rd ed., 1790). I have written on Wesley and Justification in *Wesley and Men Who Followed* (Edinburgh: Banner of Truth Trust, 2003), pp. 217-31.

redemption was gaining influence in Wales in the nineteenth century, it was Hurrion's sermons on Particular Redemption which were translated into Welsh and published in 1820, with a Preface by John Elias. Elias, the evangelical leader in North Wales, regretted they had not been published earlier:

> These sermons were highly prized by the defenders and lovers of the truth in London for scores of years, but were hidden from monoglot Welshmen until the present year. There has been, and still is, great anger in the world against the Doctrines of Grace.[13]

At times controversy over universal redemption has sometimes been diverted from Scripture by criticism of the advocates or opponents of the teaching. It is a merit of Hurrion's exposition in these pages that personalities do not figure in his treatment. About to enter eternity, he was occupied with a higher concern. Nor did he question the Christian standing of all with whom he disagreed. He knew that controversy about grace which lacks grace is destructive. Although there is clearer light with some Christians than with others, humility becomes all for 'if any man think that he knoweth anything,

[13] For the development of the controversy in North Wales, through the influence of Edward Williams, see 'John Elias' in Iain H. Murray, *Seven Leaders: Preachers and Pastors* (Edinburgh: Banner of Truth Trust, 2017), pp. 27-38. The Elias Preface is reproduced below. Translated from the Welsh by John Aaron, it first appeared in *Banner of Truth* (Nov. 2016), which issue also addresses the teaching of Moise Amyraut (or Amyrald) by whom both Baxter and Williams were influenced. 'Williams did not realize that in moderating Calvinism he was setting in motion a process over the development of which he would have no control. ... Eventually it was taken to a point where Calvinism had virtually been abandoned altogether.' W. T. Owen, *Edward Williams, 1750-1813* (Cardiff: University Press, 1963), pp. 149-50.

he knoweth nothing yet as he ought to know' (1 Cor. 8:2). Whitefield was of that spirit when he noted 'Baxter's *Call to the Unconverted*' among the books which 'much benefited me', adding, 'as soon as the love of God was shed abroad in my soul, I loved all of whatsoever denomination, who loved the Lord Jesus Christ in sincerity of heart'.[14] Where devotion to Christ is uppermost brotherly love can be maintained even when believers disagree.

Certainly diligence in contending for the faith is never to be suspended, and these pages are reprinted in the prayerful hope of a greater recovery of biblical truth today.

IAIN H. MURRAY
Edinburgh
March 2017

---

[14] Whitefield's *Journals*, p. 62.

Preface[1]

Gentle Reader

The following sermons on redemption were composed by the Rev. John Hurrion a little before his death. He preached the first two sermons at Lime Street, as one of the various divines who preached there on different aspects of the doctrines of grace; doctrines which were being denied by many at that time. He was prevented by illness and death from preaching the last two. In his illness he prepared the third sermon for the press, and wrote the text of the fourth which he entrusted to a friend to oversee its publication. These sermons were highly prized by the defenders and lovers of the truth in London for scores of years, but were hidden from monoglot Welshmen until the present day. It is a great joy to me to see them now translated carefully into the Welsh language, and I hope they shall prove to be of great blessing to my country.[2]

[1] This introduction by John Elias (translated by John Aaron) is taken from a Welsh edition of Hurrion's four sermons: *A Defence of the Scriptural Doctrine of Particular Redemption, Set Out and Affirmed, in Four Sermons, Preached at Lime Street, London, by the Rev. John Hurrion, a Minister of the Nonconformists. Together with a Short Account of the Life of the Author. Translated into Welsh by Evan Evans.*

[2] The translator Evan Evans (1795–1855) was born into a Calvinistic Methodist family but was ordained into the Church of England. He was a curate in Chester and Rhyl. He is known under his pen-name Ieuan Glan Geirionydd as a writer of

The doctrine presented and defended here is of the greatest import. It contains the sum and substance of the gospel. If this branch of the doctrines of grace were removed from the gospel it might be said that it would be *another* gospel, *which is not another*, that is, it would not be a gospel: the doctrine would not be to the glory of God, nor of comfort to any feeling sinner.

There has been, and still is, great anger in the world against the doctrines of grace, and this branch of the teaching has been as much the target of the arrows of the enemies of the truth as any other branch, if not more so. The wisdom of this world and fleshly reason have gathered all their armies and armouries against it; the gates of hell, in many forms, have sought to pursue it out of this world, but 'they have not prevailed'.

The Lord has raised godly instruments, simple and appropriate, in every age to defend it, and by blessing them he has not left himself without witness. And one of the faithful witnesses for the truth of this branch of doctrine was the godly author of the following sermons. The truth has been handled with such light and clarity, and the counter-arguments against the truth have been answered so fairly and solidly, and the consequences of denying the truth been displayed as so vile, that no impartial seeker of the truth can do less than be confirmed, built up and satisfied as he reads; and the

---

fine hymns, many still sung in Welsh. He also translated Boston's *Fourfold State of Man* into Welsh.

applications are so evangelical and sweet that the most fearful and disheartened Christian can do no less than be comforted.

Since the beginning of the revival in Wales (associated with Harris, Rowland, etc.) until very recently, there have been very few among the Nonconformists (especially in north Wales) who have denied this doctrine. But presently, to the grief of all who love the truth as it is in Jesus, there are some who, like the Morganites and Half-Morganites[3] of old, seek to preach and write insolently and shamelessly against it. There is some concern in Wales because of the Morganites, but the Half-Morganites are the more dangerous, and more probable of causing damage; indeed, they corrupt many. They wrap themselves up in a most hypocritical cloak, pretending to be very zealous for the truth and to be seeking to reconcile fleshly reason and the doctrines of grace. But as they seek to mediate between the two, they turn themselves to the side of the flesh, speaking deceitfully and shamelessly against the truth. And no branch of the truth receives more wrong from them than that discussed in these sermons, namely redemption. They seek to destroy this doctrine by omitting, or denying, the greatest matters involved in it, namely, Christ's commitment in the eternal covenant to redeem sinners from the curse of the law, and from the wrath of God; the establishment of him by his Father in their place; the accounting of their sins to him; the full punishment that they deserved being suffered

---

[3] 'Morganites' was the Welsh term for Pelagians, in that there was a tradition in Wales that Pelagius was a Welsh monk called Morgan. 'Half-Morganites', presumably, is Elias's term for Semi-Pelagians.

by him; his perfect atonement for them, and the gaining of certain salvation for them, etc., etc.

But they fail to drive this truth out of the Bible, and fail to twist the Bible to witness against it, or to testify in favour of their new doctrine. And in that there are no weapons to be found in the realm of orthodox theology, or in the armoury of the holy Scriptures, to defend their doctrine, they form strange new words not previously known to our nation. That doctrine must be weak and unscriptural that requires the invention of new phrases to defend and maintain it. But 'no man also having drunk old wine straightway desireth new: for he saith, The old is better'.

I am very pleased that one of the godly servants of the Nonconformists has been called, as one from the dead, to witness for the doctrine of redemption as it is revealed in God's word. His witness is so clear and scriptural that I hope that Welsh Christians will, in general, hold to it, and be strengthened by it; and, without doubt, it is surely the clear words of Scripture that are best to witness for the truth; there is no need for obscure words and philosophical arguments to defend any branch of the doctrines of grace.

Now, reader, let me not keep you any longer at the door, but allow you to enter into the precious chambers of the truth handled in the following sermons. I desire not only that you should agree with the truth being stated but that your soul also should enjoy a spiritual feast and divine edification by these truths. I believe, with certainty, that there is no other view of the doctrine of redemption able to satisfy the soul that has been brought to know God, and the law, and his own condition through the Fall. In this doctrine my soul finds the means of life and the means also of dying in comfort. I am, reader, loving the glory of the Redeemer and your own eternal welfare, your servant in the gospel,

JOHN ELIAS
Llanfechell
July 20, 1820

Sermon 1

TITUS 2:14.—Jesus Christ gave himself for us, that he might redeem us from all iniquity, and purify to himself a peculiar people, zealous of good works.

THIS chapter begins with Paul's instructions to Titus, to speak the things which become sound doctrine, or to press on several ranks of persons such duties, as would adorn the doctrine of God their Saviour, which doctrine is next specified in several important branches of it; such as the doctrine of salvation by grace, and of the celestial glory called the *blessed hope*; the doctrine of Christ's deity, and second glorious coming to judgment; and the doctrine of our redemption by the death of Christ, with the end and design of it, verses 11, 13, 14.

This last mentioned is the subject which falls to my share in this Lecture; which I shall the more cheerfully insist upon, because I find it to be one of those important points, with respect to which the apostle gave Titus a charge to 'speak, and exhort, and rebuke, with all authority', verse 15, as if he had said, Do thou declare these doctrines, and exhort the hearers to receive them; and rebuke, with all authority, or powerfully convince and reprove gainsayers, in such a manner, as none may despise thee.

The doctrine of our redemption by Christ, I take to be fully contained in the words of my text, 'Christ gave himself for us, that he might redeem us from all iniquity, and purify to himself a peculiar people, zealous of good works.'

Before I come to discourse directly on this doctrine, I shall premise two things.

1. I shall consider the *extent* of Christ's redemption, or the persons to whom it belongs, as represented in my text.

2. I shall shew the *weight* and *importance* of this doctrine.

1st, I am to consider the *extent* of this redemption, or the persons to whom it belongs, as represented in my text.

To state this right, we are to observe that the question is not whether there is an infinite merit and worth in Christ's redeeming blood: This both parties readily allow. Nor is it a matter in debate whether *many*, or only a *few* persons are redeemed by Christ, seeing they are said in scripture, Rev. 5:9, to be 'a great multitude that no man could number, of all nations, and kindreds, and people, and tongues'. But the true state of the question is this: Whether according to the will of the Father, and the intention of the Son, Christ died to reconcile and save all men, or a select chosen number only; the latter is what we affirm, and our opponents deny.

Let us now see how this matter is represented in my text, and which sentiment is approved and confirmed thereby.

Christ 'gave himself to redeem us', or, by an expiatory sacrifice, to deliver us from sin and misery, and make us eternally happy. 'He redeemed us from the curse, being made a curse for us', Gal. 3:13. 'He redeemed those that were under the law, that they might receive the adoption of sons.' The persons redeemed are more generally specified by the word *us*; which is a word often used, in scripture, to signify the elect and believers; as where it is said, 'God has not appointed *us* to wrath, but to obtain salvation through Jesus Christ, who died for us that we might live together with him', 1 Thess. 5:9, 10. The redeemed people are also represented, in my text, as those who, in due time, are *redeemed from all iniquity*, or from the guilt and power, and the very being of all sin; and also as purified to Christ, or really sanctified, and made holy, changed into his image, and fitted for fellowship and communion with himself. The redeemed are said to be a *peculiar people*; they are Christ's jewels, his treasure, distinguished from others in his intention, purchase, esteem, and care; they are a *chosen generation*, and therefore a *peculiar* or *purchased people*, 1 Pet. 2:9, they are the travail of Christ's soul, the dear offspring of his blood, whom he loved, and therefore *gave himself for them*.—The redeemed are also represented as persons *zealous of good works*, works of faith and love, and of repentance and new obedience; such works as have a divine life for the principle of them, a divine direction for their rule, even the revealed will of God, and a divine attainment for the end, that is, the glory of God. To be zealous of these good works,

3

is to love them fervently, to perform them diligently, and to promote them with industry and vigour.

According to this account of the redeemed people, let us see whether we are to believe that Christ gave himself to redeem all men, or a select and peculiar number only. In my text, Christ is said to give himself *for us*, in our room and stead, to satisfy offended justice for all those whose iniquities were laid upon him, and for whom he died. Now, did Christ stand in the stead of all men? Did he satisfy divine justice for the sins of millions, who yet suffer the vengeance of eternal fire, for the same sins themselves? Or did Christ make satisfaction for a peculiar number only, who shall never come into condemnation, but enjoy eternal life, as the purchase and fruit of his death?

When it is said that *Christ gave himself, that he might redeem to himself a peculiar people*, can the meaning be, that he died to render the salvation of all men possible? Or, is it not rather meant, that he died to render the salvation of a select number certain and perfect? Can we suppose that Christ died to render the salvation of all men possible, when multitudes were actually in hell, and so beyond any possibility of salvation, at the very time when Christ suffered? The reply made to this will be considered and confuted hereafter. Does not the scripture speak of the effects and fruits of Christ's death, not as mere possibilities, but as things real and certain? 'He shall see his seed, the travail of his soul,' Isa. 53:10, 11. Does not Christ say, that *he laid down his life for his sheep, that they should never perish,* but *he would give them eternal life?* John 10:28.

If Christ died to purchase to himself such as should be *a purified people, zealous of good works,* then surely he did not give himself to redeem all men, those who are never purified, as well as those that are: if he gave himself for a peculiar people, then not for all people; if for those who, in time, are made zealous of good works, then surely not for those who live and die enemies to good works, and zealous against them.

If Christ gave himself for a peculiar people, whom he valued as his *jewels* and *treasure,* and *who shall be his when he makes up his jewels,* then he did not give himself for all men; for all men are not his jewels and treasure, or peculiar people, Mal. 3:16, seeing that in the day when he makes up his jewels, there shall be a manifest difference between his jewels and others, between the righteous and the wicked, those that fear God, and those that fear him not.

If these things are calmly and carefully considered, one would think that any impartial and understanding person may be able to determine whether Christ, in giving himself, did intend to redeem all men, or a chosen and peculiar number only: If the latter is the true sense of the text, as it appears to me, we might rest here, and seek no farther evidence; for the scriptures do not contradict themselves, the Spirit of truth cannot err or deceive us.

But it may here be objected, that the redemption by Christ is as extensive as the grace of the Father; but the grace of the

Father appeared to all men, Titus 2:11, therefore the redemption of the Son extends to all men. Here we shall readily allow, that Christ redeemed all men, in as extensive a sense, as the grace of God is said to have appeared to all men: For multitudes in the world, before the writing this epistle, at that time, and since, neither had, nor even now have, any discovery of this grace to them. The *all men* then to whom it appeared, must mean only *some* of all sorts; and so makes nothing for the doctrine of universal grace, or universal redemption. In the context, the apostle had been speaking of the duties of aged men and women, of young men and young women, and of servants to their masters; to which he excited them, by the consideration of that grace which has appeared to all men, or to persons of all ranks and stations, and obliges them to adorn the doctrine of God their Saviour: But what argument can be drawn from thence for universal redemption?

It may be said, the several parts of the text have been urged in favour of particular redemption; and it must be owned, that as to the event and effect, the redemption is not, cannot be universal, seeing all are not saved from sin, and purified; yet the purpose, design, and intention of Christ in giving himself, might extend to all men, though all men are not actually saved. To which I reply, that my text declares the purpose, design, and intention of Christ in giving himself, even to redeem from all iniquity, and purify to himself a peculiar people: Can this mean all men? Did Christ intend, in laying down his life, to sanctify and save all men? If so,

6

then Christ is frustrated and disappointed of his end: How then does the *pleasure of the Lord prosper in his hands*? How does he *see his seed, the travail of his soul*? or how does *he give eternal life to as many as the Father gave him*? If Christ's intention in giving himself was to redeem and save all men, and only some men are saved, how could it be said, *he shall be satisfied*? Isa. 53:11. Could Christ be satisfied to have his intention disappointed, and his promise fail, when he said, 'If I be lifted up, I will draw all men to me', John 12:32? Or what satisfaction could he take in seeing the scripture broke, which says, 'He shall not fail nor be discouraged' Isa. 42:4, or in seeing the will of the Father, that 'he should lose nothing of all that were given him', frustrated and made void? Where does the scripture speak of Christ's death, and the ends of it in terms of uncertainty, or represent him as coming short of his aim and intention, in dying for sinners? This does not appear to me to be a scripture doctrine, but an invention of men, framed to support an hypothesis, which they are fond of: But till some scripture evidence is brought to support it, we may justly reject it.—But I proceed to the next thing proposed.

2*dly*, I shall shew the *weight* and *importance* of this doctrine, relating to the extent of Christ's redemption.

It must be obvious, to every diligent enquirer into these things, how prone men generally are to run into extremes, in this, as well as in other things. Some look upon all enquiries of this nature as vain and useless; and others are so much taken up with them, as to neglect other weighty doctrines, or duties of the Christian religion. The conduct of each sort is blameable and carefully to be avoided. With what view and design Christ laid down his precious life, is, whatever some think, a point of very great moment, with regard to the sense of many scriptures, the glory of Christ, and of the divine perfections, the encouragement of faith, and the comfort and establishment of believers, as may more fully appear hereafter. A clear decision of the controversy upon this bond, must be allowed to be of very great service towards the removal of the heavy imputations with which the contending parties lend each other's scheme, and to allay our heats, and remove our divisions, that we might 'stand fast in one spirit, striving together for the faith of the gospel', against the common enemy, who is sapping and subverting the very foundations of it.

A late writer[1] has had the confidence to tell the world, in print, that the training up his apostles was the work, or the main work that God had given Christ to do; and that it was his principal design, in giving up himself a sacrifice, that he might enable them by his death, and what would follow it, his resurrection, ascension, and the sending of the Holy Ghost, to preach, with success, and spread his kingdom in the world: 'What words', says our author, 'can well raise our idea of the office of the apostles higher, than that Jesus lived and died, to prepare them for the due discharge of that trust?'

[1] The Lord Barrington, in his *Miscellanea Sacra*, II:76, 77.

We may add, what words can sink our idea of Christ's office lower, or cover the design of his death with more disgrace? If Christ's principal design in giving up himself a sacrifice, was to prepare the apostles for the true discharge of their work, we need not trouble ourselves about the general or special ends of his death, whether he gave himself to redeem all men, or some only; nor much concern ourselves with what the apostle meant, by Christ's giving himself to redeem from all iniquity, and purify to himself a peculiar people, zealous of good works; seeing, according to our author, this was not Christ's principal end and intention, in dying, to save men; but to set up the apostles above himself, and obtain a kingdom by their means. It is very strange that the apostle should forget all this dignity, to which Christ, by his death, had advanced him, and not say one word of it, in the account which he gives us of the end and design of Christ's death. Farther, to what purpose are we told that Christ gave himself for us, to reconcile and bring us to God, that he purchased the church with his own blood, and obtained eternal redemption for us, and washed us from our sins in his own blood? How little reason had the church to adore and praise him for this, if the chief business of his life and death was to procure apostles, to preach the gospel, and advance his kingdom in the world!

Forasmuch then as things are come to this pass among us, and the intention and design of Christ's death is not only mistaken by some, as to the number of the redeemed, but, which is infinitely worse, seeing it is so openly and impiously perverted and denied by others, it is high time to make a strict enquiry into this matter, and, if possible, to find out and establish the true end and design of Christ's death, according to the scripture account thereof: And especially, seeing the sacred writings speak so much of it, and lay such a stress upon it, with regard to the glory of God, and the salvation of men. And it ought to be considered, whether the rendering the end of Christ's death so precarious to all, and the allowing, as some must do, the disappointment of his intention therein to so many, has not tempted many to run the desperate length of denying all its atoning virtue and salutary effects. If this is found to be true, of what importance must it be to understand and hold fast the true design and intention of Christ, in giving himself to redeem sinners? More, I think, need not be added, as to the importance of the point in hand; I shall therefore throw what I have to say upon it under two heads.

I. I shall endeavour to establish and confirm the doctrine of particular redemption, in several distinct propositions; and shall make plain deductions from them.

II. I shall answer the principal arguments, and vindicate the chief passages of scripture produced in opposition thereto.

I. I shall *confirm* and *establish* the doctrine of *particular redemption*; or prove that Christ did not give himself to redeem all men, but to redeem and actually save, a chosen and peculiar number: This, which I take to be the truth, I shall endeavour to prove, under several distinct propositions.

1. The *Father's election*, and the *Son's redemption*, are of the same extent, or relate to the same individual persons, to all such, and to none else: All the chosen people are redeemed, and all the redeemed are chose to salvation, 'through the sprinkling of the blood of Jesus', 1 Pet. 1:2.

The life which Christ procured by his death, and which he applies by his Spirit, is by him bestowed on those very persons whom the Father had given him: He said of himself thus: 'That he should give eternal life to as many as thou hast given him', John 17:2, which words are restrictive and plainly limited to the elect, whom the Father gave to Christ to redeem by his death: And thus election and redemption answer each other. Christ being made perfect, through sufferings, brings the many sons to glory, and presents them to the Father, saying, 'Behold I, and the children which God hath given me', Heb. 2:10, 13. Those given to Christ, and brought to glory by him, are those for whom he was made perfect through sufferings, so exact an agreement is there between the Father's choice, and the Son's purchase: They both pursue the same intention, and each person does his part to make the same individual persons happy. Hence it is said, 'Who shall lay any thing to the charge of God's elect? It is God that justifies; who is he that condemns? It is Christ that died', Rom. 8:33, 34. Seeing Christ died for the elect, and God the Father justifies those for whom Christ died, who shall condemn them, whom the

Father has chosen, and the Son has redeemed, by his most precious blood?

Christ has told us in express terms, that 'he came down from heaven to do the will of him that sent him', which will he declared to be, 'that of all which he had given him, he should lose nothing, but should raise it up at the last day', John 6:38, 39. The resurrection here spoke of shews, that they are persons which the Father gave the Son to redeem, and preserve to eternal life; none of which given and redeemed persons can be lost, because it is the Father's will that they should not; and the Son came to fulfil that will, and has assured us, that all that the Father gives him shall come to him, and that he would cast out none of them, but raise up every believer at the last day, John 6:37, 40. So exactly do the Father's election and the Son's redemption agree, with respect to the persons chosen and redeemed.

This also plainly appears, from those scripture passages: 'According as he hath chosen us in him; in whom we have redemption through his blood', Eph. 1:4, 7. They are evidently the same persons who are first said to be chosen, and then to be redeemed by the blood of Christ: so exactly commensurate is the latter to the former. And we may observe, that there is not, here or elsewhere, the least intimation that Christ's redemption either exceeds or falls short of the Father's election, in one single instance, or individual person. All who were chosen are redeemed, and all who are redeemed in time were chosen from eternity.

The same truth is signified in that scripture, 'That Jesus should die for that nation, and not for that nation only, but also that he should gather together in one the children of God that were scattered abroad', John 11:51, 52, even the elect people, dispersed throughout the world. These Christ was to draw to himself, by the virtue of his death, according to his own words; 'I, if I am lifted up [crucified] will draw all men to me', John 12:32, all those who are the sons of God by election, or, to use the apostle's phrase, who are *predestinated to the adoption of children*, Eph. 1:5.

The truth of the proposition that the Father's election and the Son's redemption are of the same extent, or that Christ died for all chosen, and those only who were given to him by the Father, I think, is fully proved by the scriptures alleged: The plain deduction and inference from which is, that Christ did not give himself to redeem all men, but a select number only.

2. Christ's redemption is *absolute*, *certain*, and *perfect*.

By its being absolute and certain, I mean, that Christ's redemption did not depend upon any previous desert in man; nor is the efficacy of it suspended upon the free will of man, so as it should be in his power to make it effectual, or ineffectual, as he pleases. This redemption is said to be perfect, with respect to the end or effect of it, that is, the perfect happiness of all the redeemed, who are freed from all sin, and all the penal consequences of it.

We have been often told, that Christ died *conditionally* for *all men*, but *absolutely* for *no man*; that he procured reconciliation and remission of sins for all men, and yet it might have so happened, as that not one person should have enjoyed either pardon or peace with God, seeing, as some say, Christ left it to men, to embrace or refuse the atonement, as they pleased: But Christ himself asserts, that *all that the Father gave him shall come to him*, John 6:37. How low and mean a notion of redemption is it to say, that Christ made only a conditional purchase, and left it in the power of man to render it effectual, by believing, or to make it null and void by unbelief, as he would! How much this opinion tends to exalt the power and pride of the sinner, and to depreciate the love and redemption of Christ, one would think must be evident to every intelligent person at the first view. That without faith no man can enjoy eternal redemption is certain; but that Christ has left it to men to make void the ends of his death, and the intention of his redeeming love, as they please, is contrary to scripture, and all good sense. Faith is not of a man's self, it is *the gift of God*, Eph. 2:8, but it is also the purchase of Christ's blood, and is certainly wrought in the hearts of the redeemed by the Holy Spirit, on the account of the Father's election and Christ's redemption, Titus 1:1, therefore it is styled 'the faith of God's elect, obtained through the righteousness of God our Saviour', 2 Pet. 1:1. Hence Christ said, that *his sheep shall hear his voice*, John 10:16. Christ spoke not doubtfully, but with certainty and resolution; he did not say, they shall hear my voice, if they will; if not, I submit my will and my work to their will and pleasure. As Christ died for men, without asking their previous consent, so he makes them *willing in the day of his power*, Psa. 110:3, and renders his redemption certainly effectual to all those persons, and for all those ends, for which he gave himself. When it is said, that 'Christ is entered into heaven for us, having obtained eternal redemption for us, by his blood', Heb. 9:12, 24, can any thing less be meant, than that Christ, having made a perfect, and absolute purchase of salvation, by his death, ascended to heaven, to appear in the presence of God for the redeemed, and to secure their actual and eternal enjoyment of that salvation? If it be said, that Christ obtained redemption for all such as will have it, it must be granted; but then none will have it, but such as God makes willing, as he certainly does all his elect, and none else.

The scriptures speak of the intention and effect of Christ's death, in the most absolute and certain terms; 'When enemies, we were reconciled to God, by the death of his Son, and shall much more be saved by his life', Rom. 5:10. 'He died for us, that we should live together with him', 1 Thess. 5:10; 'God hath appointed us to obtain salvation by Jesus Christ', verse 9, or actually to enjoy it. What obstacles lay in the way, Christ undertook to remove; whatever is necessary to fit the redeemed for glory, he will see accomplished, and never leave his sheep, for whom he laid down his life, John 10:28, nor part with them out of his hand, but will bring them all safe to heaven: He has given us his word for it, that they shall never perish, but he will give them eternal life. Christ gave himself for us, to redeem us from all iniquity, absolutely, not conditionally, if we would; but he gave himself, with resolution to carry the work through, and make it effectual: This, I think, is plainly the sense of my text.

I cannot forbear digressing so far, as to observe what a glorious redemption this is, worthy of him that contrived it, and of him that procured it, and infinitely superior to that conditional redemption, which subjects the will and merits of Christ to the caprice and humour of sinners, and represents him as a well meaning, but weak Redeemer, who intended to save all men, but could not accomplish his design, by reason of men's not doing their part. According to our opponents, Christ's purchase respected his Father rather than men; it, as they say, procured God a right and power to save men on what conditions he pleased; so that when it is said, that God was reconciled, it is only meant that he was reconcilable, and Christ did not procure salvation, but only a salvability; he was but a titular Saviour, a Saviour without salvation, and a Redeemer without redemption: Christ is only the remote cause, but man the immediate cause; Christ the potential, but man the actual cause of his own redemption: Is this honourable to Christ?

If Christ died conditionally for all men, to save them, provided they would believe and repent, the question is, Whether he procured these conditions, repentance and faith, for all men; if not, how shall they come by them? If he did, why do not all receive them? seeing 'Christ is exalted to be a Prince and a Saviour, to give repentance and remission of sins'. If he does not give them, is it either for want of power, or for want of will? How can he want power, who is 'God over all, blessed for ever'; and, as Mediator, 'has all power in heaven and earth committed to him'? And if it proceeds from a want of will in Christ, that they do not receive them, how then did he intentionally redeem all men, if he withholds the conditions upon which it is suspended? If it is said, it was not agreed between the Father and the Son that these conditions should be bestowed on all men, then it was because it was not the intention of the Father and the Son, that they should receive them, and so be saved: And if it is so, then neither Father nor Son really intended that all men should be redeemed and saved; for who has resisted their will? Whatever they intended to do shall be done. The matter is not left at uncertainties; Christ's redemption is absolute, certain, and perfect: And hence it follows, that Christ did not die to redeem all men, seeing all men do not enjoy an absolute, certain, and perfect redemption.

3. Christ's *suretyship* and *sufferings* are of the *same extent*: Christ died to redeem all, and only those, whose debt he, as their surety, undertook to pay.

Christ is expressly said to be the surety of a better testament, or covenant, Heb. 7:22. But the question is, whether Christ is only a surety on God's part to us, as some affirm, or a surety on our part to God, as others assert? When God said, 'sacrifice and offering he would not'; when he declared, that he would not accept the legal sacrifices, as an atonement for the sins of men, then Christ said, 'Lo, I come, to do thy will, O God,' Psa. 40:8, i.e. I put myself in the place of thy chosen people; and, according to thy will, I will suffer in their stead, be a sacrifice for their sins, pay their debt, and redeem them from death: For this end, 'God laid upon him the iniquity of us all; the chastisement of our peace was upon him, and by his stripes we are healed', Isa. 53:6. What other reason can be given why our sins should be laid and punished upon Christ? or, why we should be healed by his stripes, but his suretyship, or standing in our place, room, and stead, and so suffering the just for the unjust, or giving his life a ransom for many? On this account, we find God the Father re-stipulating to Christ that he should 'see his seed, the travail of his soul, and should be satisfied', verse 11. There was an exact agreement between Christ's payment and purchase, between the price he paid, and the persons he redeemed; he paid the full debt of all, for whom he was surety, and he secures the eternal redemption of every one, for whom he made the payment. We could neither pay the debt which we had contracted, nor purchase the inheritance which we had forfeited, nor claim the promises which are *yea and amen, only in Christ*: It is therefore by means of his death, in our room and stead, that we 'receive the promise of the eternal inheritance', Heb. 9:15.

The grand question here is, For whom was Christ surety, whose debt did he pay, whose freedom did he procure? Let the event declare this; for certainly Christ did not die in vain, or purchase deliverance, and yet lose the price he paid, or any part of the purchase he made; for that would be contrary to all the rules of justice and righteousness. Who then are they that are delivered from the wrath to come, and shall inherit everlasting life? Is this the lot of all men, or of some only? If of some only, as matter of fact proves, then Christ was not the surety of all men; he did not die to redeem all men, but some only. If Christ had been surety of the covenant for all men, and had purchased grace and salvation for all men, then all men should certainly enjoy them, Psa. 89:33, 34, for God could not break his covenant, nor suffer his faithfulness to fail.

If it is said, that Christ died to procure and establish a covenant of grace with all mankind, and that every man is born under this covenant, and that the works of nature reveal this covenant to all men, and call all men into it; I answer, that the scriptures nowhere speak of such an universal covenant of grace, procured by Christ, or made with men. If there was such a covenant subsisting, surely it should have been revealed and made known to all men; but multitudes of persons, yea nations, never had the knowledge of this covenant. God, at first, made a distinction between the seed of the woman, and the seed of the serpent, which has been kept up ever since, Gen. 3:15. The covenant was established with Abel, and Cain was rejected; Abel being slain, Seth was raised up, as the seed of the covenant; after him, Noah and his family were taken into covenant with God, and the old world rejected and destroyed: After that, God established his covenant with Abraham, Isaac, and Jacob, whilst Ishmael and Esau were excluded. And the Jews were God's covenant people; but the rest of the nations were suffered to walk in their own ways. And, to this day, there are great numbers, not only of persons, but of nations, who never heard of Christ, or the covenant of grace, and are they yet in or under this covenant? 'How will they believe in him, of whom they have not heard?' Rom. 10:14. The works of nature, indeed, teach men many things concerning God, as a Creator, but not as a Redeemer: They discover his being, power, wisdom, goodness, and providence; but not his saving grace and good pleasure in Christ, nor Christ's merit, intercession, or government; nor can they instruct men in the nature of the covenant established upon those better promises, in the hands of a Mediator, Heb. 8:6, or discover to them the perpetuity of those promises, which are yea and amen in Christ Jesus, or that eternal life comprised in the covenant, but given only in and through the Son of God. These things were hid from ages and generations, who cannot therefore be supposed, by the works of nature, to be called into the covenant of grace.—Moreover, if all men are brought under a covenant of grace, how could the apostle speak of some 'still under the law, and under the curse', Gal. 3:10, 'children of wrath, and strangers to the covenant of promise, without Christ, without hope, and without God in the world', Eph. 2:3, 12, especially if Christ was the surety of an universal covenant?

If Christ is the surety of a covenant, which, though it includes an innumerable company, yet not all men, then he is not the surety of all men, and consequently did not die to redeem all men; for on what grounds can it be said that he died for any more, or others, than those for whom he is surety? How could he be required to die, and satisfy divine justice for any men, otherwise than as he had voluntarily put himself in their room, and had undertaken to satisfy the demands of the law and justice of God on their behalf? If Christ was the surety of an universal covenant, then he paid the debts of all men, made satisfaction for the sins of all men, otherwise he would not have fulfilled his trust, nor have been faithful either to God or man. And if he did satisfy for the sins of all men, then, in justice all men must be exempted from suffering for them, and so hell is dispeopled at once, or else a double satisfaction would be required for the same sins, which is as contrary to God's justice, as to have none at all. Upon the whole, seeing multitudes suffer the vengeance of eternal fire, for their own sins, it is evident, that Christ was not the surety of an universal covenant of grace, was not the surety of all men: and hence the conclusion clearly and strongly follows, that he did not give himself to redeem all men.

4. Christ's *oblation* and *intercession* relate to the same persons.

'He bore the sins of many, and made intercession for the transgressors', Isa. 53:12. For what transgressors? for those whose sins he bore. To offer for the sins of the people, and to pray for them, were the two main parts of the priestly office, under the law, and of Christ's priestly office, as it is represented under the gospel. 'It is Christ that died, who also makes intercession for us', Rom. 8:34. And again, 'We have an advocate with the Father, Jesus Christ the righteous, who also is the propitiation for our sins', 1 John 2:1, 2. The one answers the other: The intercession is founded upon the propitiation. There is no reason to think that Christ died for those for whom he would not intercede, or that, he interceded for any for whom he did not die; the scriptures apply both to the same persons, or speak of them as done both for the same persons. There are some for whom we are *not to pray*, 1 John 5:16, and can we think that Christ prayed for them himself? What is Christ's intercession, but a presenting to the Father that sacrifice which he had offered for the sins of men, with a desire that they may enjoy the blessings purchased thereby. Christ has told us, 'That he did not pray for the world', John 17:9, therefore he did not die for the world, as the word is taken, for all men; for if he had offered the sacrifice for all, it would bear a plea for all; and we cannot conceive that Christ should refuse to intercede for any, whom he loved so well as to bleed and die for them. If it is said, that Christ foresaw the unworthiness of the wicked world, and therefore resolved not to pray for them, it may be also said, that he foresaw the unworthiness of the wicked world, and therefore would not die for them; for what reason can be given why that wickedness and unworthiness, which is supposed to hinder Christ's praying for them, should not also hinder his dying for them.

But it may be said, Christ prayed for those that crucified him: He prayed for Jerusalem, and therefore doth not limit his intercession to the elect. I answer, that those for whom Christ prayed on the cross, were afterwards converted, and so appeared to be of the number of God's chosen; and it cannot thence be proved, that he prayed for the forgiveness of all men: if he did or does, one of those two absurdities will follow, either that the Father does not *always hear Christ*, John 11:42, or that all men shall be forgiven; both which are contrary to scripture. As to Jerusalem, Christ's words relating thereto, are not properly a prayer, but rather an act of human compassion towards the miserable. It is not to be thought that Christ would pray for what he knew could not be granted,[2] and he expressly says, 'That the things of their peace were now hid from their eyes', Luke 19:42. Besides, it might be their civil, not their eternal peace, which is spoke of; and then no argument can thence be drawn for Christ praying for the eternal salvation of any besides those given him of the Father.

[2] Or, as some think, Christ refers to his prophetic office in those words, 'O that thou hadst known at least in this thy day, the things that belong to thy peace; and how often would I have gathered thee', viz. the tendency of my ministry was to shew the way of life and peace, but ye refused instruction. *Collat. Piscat, cum Vorstio*, pp. 2, 94.

If then it holds true, that Christ intercedes only for those given him out of the world, and if he intercedes for all for whom he died, then he did not die for all men, seeing all men were not given to him by the Father; and he does not intercede for all men, not for the world, but for a peculiar number given him out of the world: A part given him out of the world, cannot mean the whole world; neither can the words of Christ, 'I pray not for the world', John 17:9, 20, be restrained to the apostles, because in the same prayer, he says, 'Neither pray I for these alone, but for those also who shall believe on me, through their word.' Christ's prayer then extends to all such, as in time believe, and to none else: therefore so does his death, seeing, as has been proved, his oblation and intercession relate to the same persons.

5. Christ did not die to procure the remission of *their* sins, whose sins he knew beforehand were irremissible; for that would have been, so far, to have died in vain. It would not have been to have done his Father's will, but to have acted in direct opposition to it, in purchasing remission for those whose sins can never be forgiven. 'The blasphemy against the Holy Ghost shall never be forgiven to men', Matt. 12:31. This Christ declared with his own mouth; and did he, after such a declaration, die to procure the pardon of their sins, who can never be forgiven? Far be it from us, to impute such a weakness and absurdity to the only wise God our Saviour. Does Christ forbid us to pray for the pardon of that sin, 1 John 5:16, and yet did he shed his blood to procure the pardon of

those that were guilty of it? And if he did not die for them, then he did not die for all men.

It will, I suppose, be generally allowed, that the sins of those actually in hell, are irremissible, for 'there the fire is never quenched, and the worm dieth not', Mark 9:43, 44, and out of that place there is no redemption. At the very time when Christ suffered, there were multitudes in that place of torment; and how absurd is it to suppose, that Christ paid the price of redemption for millions, who at that very instant, were suffering the vengeance of eternal fire for their own sins! If it is said, is it not as absurd for Christ to pay the price of their redemption, who were actually in heaven at the time of payment, and so stood in no need of it? To this we may reply, that those who were in heaven when Christ died, were admitted on the credit of that purchase, which he had undertook to make for them: but Christ could not die for the damned, upon any supposition of their deliverance and salvation; or by virtue of any engagement, on his part, to deliver them. But it may be urged, that Christ was to pay the price of the day and means of grace, and a possibility of their salvation; and this was as much due to God for those in hell, as for any out of it: To this I answer distinctly; that it nowhere appears in scripture, that Christ stood engaged to purchase a day, and means of grace, and possibility of salvation for all men; and if so, the reason of his suffering for those in hell ceaseth. Besides, it is plain, that many of the damned did never enjoy a day and means of grace; for 'God neglected and overlooked them, and suffered them to walk in their own ways', Acts 17:30. They lived without God in the world. The gospel was hid from them, and by all their natural or acquired wisdom, they knew not God, 1 Cor. 1:21; what price could Christ have to pay for such? was he to pay for what they never had? In short, Christ could not engage to procure a possibility of salvation for such as could not possibly be saved, as Cain and Judas, and such as committed the sin against the Holy Ghost: and therefore he could not die to render salvation possible to all men.

The deduction from the whole is, that Christ did not intend, by his death, to reconcile and save all men, or to render the salvation of all men possible; seeing he well knew, that the salvation of some men was, when he died, impossible; and that they never had enjoyed a day or means of grace or salvation, nor had he undertaken to purchase it for them.

6. Those for whom Christ died, are *exempted from condemnation*, and shall at last be presented to God with exceeding joy.

The apostle Paul puts this question, 'Who is he that condemneth? it is Christ that died', Rom. 8:34. This is spoke indefinitely, and belongs to all for whom Christ died; for the apostle puts no guard or limitation upon it. Through Christ's blood 'there is redemption, the forgiveness of sins, according to the riches of God's grace', Eph. 1:7. But if multitudes, for whom Christ's blood was shed, never enjoy that forgiveness, then it is not according to the riches of grace, nor indeed according to the strict rules of justice. If any, and especially if the greater part of those, for whom Christ died, are, notwithstanding, eternally condemned, how weak must the apostle's reasoning be, and how groundless and vain his challenge! 'Who is he that condemneth? it is Christ that died', Rom. 8:34. On the other hand, if Christ's death exempts all men from condemnation, for whom he died, then his reasoning is just and strong, but then it will thence follow, that he did not die for all men, seeing so many are eternally condemned.

Christ shall see the travail of his soul, and shall be satisfied, and shall hereafter present the redeemed to the Father, with exceeding joy; saying, 'Behold I, and the children which God hath given me', Heb. 2:13. Now, if Christ gave himself for all, and only a remnant are saved, what satisfaction, what joy, can he have, in presenting them to his Father? Instead of saying, 'Here am I, the children whom thou hast given me, the whole world redeemed by my blood'; may we not rather apprehend him saying, 'Behold, here is a handful, a small part of those whom I died to redeem; the rest are lost, though it was, O Father, thy will and my intention to save them all, yet their will prevailed against thine and mine, and my blood was shed for the greater number in vain.' Could this be agreeable to Christ? would this be his seeing the travail of his soul, and being satisfied? what joy could attend the presenting a small part of the redeemed to the Father? But if all for whom Christ died safely arrive in glory, then Christ may be abundantly satisfied, and joy may run through the whole celestial court. It will be a joy to the Father who chose them, to the Son who redeemed them, to the Holy Spirit who fitted them for heaven, to the holy angels who ministered to them, and to the saved themselves, that they are all there; not one lost or missing: and this, according to the scriptures, will be the real event, and true state of the case.

The plain deduction or inference from these premises, is this; that Christ did not intend, by his death, to redeem all men; for then he could not with so much joy present to the Father only a part of them, as the travail of his soul, or purchase of his blood.

The rest of the propositions to be laid down and confirmed, I must refer to my next discourse; and I shall now conclude with this one short reflection upon the whole: That the doctrine which tends most to debase man and exalt Christ, to take away boasting from us and to set forth the glory of God, that is the true doctrine of Christ's redemption: for to this end is he made redemption to us, 'That he that glories, may glory in the Lord', 1 Cor. 1:31.

Sermon 2

TITUS 2:14.—Jesus Christ gave himself for us, that he might redeem us from all iniquity, and purify to himself a peculiar people, zealous of good works.

THE gospel doctrine of our redemption by Christ, tends much to the glory of God, and the happiness of man; it is the admiration of angels, and the envy of devils. Satan, provoked to the last degree, to see man delivered out of his kingdom of darkness and misery, has left no means unattempted, to render that redemption ineffectual, as to the application of it; the purchase of which he could not prevent: for this end lie has raised up some to deny the deity of the Redeemer, and to place him in the rank of mere creatures, that so they might make void his merit and satisfaction; and, so at one blow, destroy all real redemption by Christ, pluck the crown from his head, and lay our hopes of happiness expiring with the merit and honour of the Saviour. Others, who do not deny Christ's merit and satisfaction, preclude themselves from the benefit thereof, by setting up a depraved and false medium of application instead of the true one: and here Satan has put men upon running into two dangerous extremes;

some place faith in a persuasion of the love of Christ, and of their interest in redemption by him: others rest in that faith, which only receives Christ as the true Messiah, or the Saviour that was to come into the world: and thus the devils believe, and yet tremble at the thoughts of their future doom. There is a third sort, with whom is my present concern, who, in extending Christ's redemption to all men, represent it as precarious and uncertain to all, and certainly ineffectual to the greater part of mankind, seeing such multitudes fall short of personal redemption and salvation. I might mention a fourth sort, who from the doctrine of universal redemption, draw a confident, though groundless conclusion, that they shall be saved whatever their faith or practice be, forgetting or denying my text, which asserts, that 'Christ gave himself to redeem from all iniquity, and purify to himself a peculiar people, zealous of good works'; and that therefore such as allow themselves in evil works, indulge iniquity, and are not purified, have no claim to redemption by Christ. By what has been said it appears, how Satan has been endeavouring to subvert our redemption, by his attempts upon the author of it, Christ; the instrument of its application, faith; and by misleading us, as to the objects or extent of it. It concerns us therefore to be sober and vigilant, lest our great adversary prevails against us, in any of the forementioned methods, to be injurious to the Redeemer and to our own souls.

To establish, what I take to be, the true doctrine of redemption, That Christ gave himself to redeem and save a chosen and peculiar number only, several arguments were formerly offered; it was proved, that election and redemption are of the same extent, or do relate to the same individual persons; and that therefore, seeing all are not chosen, all are not redeemed; Christ's redemption is absolute and certain; he cannot fail nor miss of the end and design of his death; and therefore the end and design of it was not to redeem and save all men, seeing all men are not redeemed and saved. Christ's surety-ship and sufferings are of the same extent; the former being the ground of the latter: but Christ is not the surety of all men; and therefore he did not suffer and die for all men. The oblation and intercession of Christ relate to the same persons; seeing then he does not intercede for all men, he did not die for all men: Nor is it to be supposed that Christ died to pro-cure the remission of their sins, whose sins were irremissible; such as the sins of the damned, and the sin against the Holy Ghost; therefore he did not die for all men: he did not die to procure remission for those actually in hell at the time of his death, or of those on earth, concerning whom his own lips had declared that they should never be forgiven, neither in this world, nor in the world to come. I further argued, that the redeemed are exempted from condemnation, and shall be presented to God with exceeding joy; but all men are not exempted from condemnation; nor shall all men be presented to God with exceeding joy: therefore Christ did not give himself to redeem all men, but a select and chosen number only. These things were more largely insisted on in my preceding discourse, under six distinct propositions: I now proceed to a seventh.

7. There is a strict and inviolable connexion between *Christ's sufferings* and his *saving benefits*. All those for whom Christ died, shall be saved by his death; every person shall enjoy eternal redemption, for whom Christ obtained it.

As God gives, so Christ purchased grace and glory, for all the redeemed; therefore, 'if when we were enemies, we were reconciled to God, by the death of his Son; much more being reconciled, we shall be saved by his life', Rom. 5:10. Christ will perfect his work; and the same persons who were reconciled by his death, shall be brought to eternal salvation by his life. His intercession in heaven secures the eternal salvation of all those for whom he gave himself an atoning sacrifice, to reconcile them to God. The purchase and application of redemption are of the same extent.

Our opponents, directly contrary to the cited scripture, teach, that multitudes of those who were reconciled to God by Christ's death, yet shall not, or will not be saved by his life. What then becomes of the apostle's argument for the certainty of men's salvation, drawn from Christ's dying for them, if many for whom he died may, and must come short of salvation; if when Christ had reconciled them by his death, they shall not certainly be saved by his life? 'If when we were enemies, we were reconciled to God, by the death of his Son, much more [says the apostle, much less, say our opponents] shall we be saved by his life.' If Christ paid the price of redemption when we were enemies, and atoned God, much more God being atoned, and a sufficient price of our redemption being paid, shall our eternal salvation be secured by Christ's life in heaven, where he appears, in the presence of God for us, and pleads the merits of his death for their salvation, whom he reconciled to God thereby. He is too wise, and too kind to those who were the travail of his soul, to lose any of them. Hence he said, 'Father, I will [I claim it as my due] that those whom thou hast given me may be with me where I am; that they may behold my glory', John 17:24.

Would any wise man pay down a valuable consideration for that which he had no assurance he should enjoy, or rather, which he knew beforehand he should never enjoy? But so it seems Christ, the wisdom of the Father, must be supposed to do, rather than infringe upon free will, and man's sovereign power in his own salvation. However, according to the scriptures, Christ did not die in vain; there is a certain connexion between reconciliation and salvation: Christ's chastisement, and their peace for whom he suffered; his stripes, and their healing for whom he was wounded, are inseparably joined together. 'The chastisement of our peace was upon him, and by his stripes we are healed', Isa. 53:5, said the prophet: But according to our opponents, our peace and healing do not certainly follow Christ's chastisement and stripes. Now, whether God or man is to be believed, let every one who is impartial judge. It is farther written, 'By his knowledge shall my righteous servant justify many, for he shall bear their iniquities', verse 11. Such are justified by Christ, whose iniquities he bore; that is, suffered and satisfied for in his death: To this agree those words of the apostle, 'He was delivered for our offences, and raised again for our justification', Rom. 4:25. What a strict connexion is there all along, between Christ's sufferings, and his saving benefits! and how are the same persons pointed out, as enjoying the salutary effects of Christ's death, for whom he suffered it!

The apostle argues, that 'he who spared not his own Son, but gave him up for us all, shall with him freely give us all things', Rom. 8:32. That is, all such for whom Christ died, shall enjoy all the saving benefits and fruits of his death, such as effectual calling, justification, and eternal glory, before-mentioned. God having given up his Son to die for us, will with him give us freely the means of grace, grace itself, and the heavenly glory, verse 30. For that love to our persons which inclined God to give his own Son, the Son of himself, of his own nature, will also dispose him to give all inferior blessings, for a double reason; partly because this Son was too great and precious a gift to be lost or given for nothing, to be given to such sufferings as he endured, and yet lose millions of souls redeemed by his blood; and also because justice required, that when the Son had paid the price of redemption, he should enjoy the purchase, or things purchased, even those for whom God gave him up: And in order thereto, God will give them all things necessary to their salvation.[1] The argument from the cited scripture lies thus; If God, having given up his Son to die for us, will with him freely give us grace and glory, then there is an inseparable connexion between Christ's sufferings, and his saving benefits: but God freely, and without any condition gave us Christ, and with him all things; therefore there is an inseparable connexion between Christ's sufferings, and his saving benefits, between his being given up for us, and the giving of all things (grace and glory purchased by Christ) to all those for whom he died.

All the parts of the argument Christ himself has given us in one discourse, leaving it to us to put them together. Christ first described the persons for whom he died, in these words, 'I lay down my life for the sheep', John 10:15. He next declared the certain effect of his laying down his life for them; 'they hear his voice and follow him', verse 27. And then he draws the conclusion, 'I give to them eternal life, and they shall never perish.' Those for whom Christ laid down his life, in time hear his voice, and follow him, and shall enjoy eternal life, as the fruit and purchase of his death for them. And thus from Christ's own words, the truth of our proposition appears; that there is an inviolable connexion, between Christ's sufferings

---

[1] One of the ancients upon these words thus expresseth himself: 'He excepts nothing who is the author of all; art thou afraid of thy Judge? consider who he is, namely, Christ, to whom the Father has committed all judgment: Can he damn thee, who redeemed thee by his death, for whom he offered himself, and whose life he knows to be the reward of his death? will he not say, What profit is there in my blood, if I condemn him whom I have died to save?'—Ambros. lib. I. *de Jacob et vita beata.* cap. 6.

and his saving benefits, and that all those for whom Christ died, shall certainly be saved.

This truth may be confirmed by other scripture testimonies: As for instance, from what is said of Christ, that 'he died for us, that whether we wake or sleep we should live together with him'. This was Christ's intention and design, that all those for whom he died should live with him in glory: either then Christ must be disappointed, or else they must for ever live with him for whom he died. Christ gave his 'flesh for the life of the world', John 6:51, and he giveth life to the same world, verse 33. The purchase, and the application of salvation are spoke of, with the same certainty, and in the same extent: There is not the least intimation, that he purchased salvation for all, but applies it only to some; the same world for whom he died, to that world he gives life; but he does not give life to *all* men; therefore by the world, Christ did not mean all men, but all those throughout the world, who believe on him, for whom he gave his flesh, to purchase their life.

We are assured, that 'God was in Christ reconciling the world unto himself, not imputing their trespasses to them; for he has made him to be sin for us, who knew no sin, that we might be made the righteousness of God in him', 2 Cor. 5:19, 21. Here we may observe, that those whom God reconciles to himself, are those to whom God does not impute trespasses; those to whom God does not impute their trespasses, are those for whom Christ was made sin, are those who are made the righteousness of God in him: Therefore, the non-imputation of sin, and the imputation of righteousness, belong to all, and only those for whom Christ was made sin, and whom God was in him reconciling to himself.

We are told, that Christ, 'by his own blood, entered in once into the holy place, having obtained eternal redemption for us', Heb. 9:12, 14, 15, that his blood purges our consciences from dead works; and that by means of his death, they which are called receive the promise of an eternal inheritance. If Christ's death obtained redemption, if it purges the conscience, and secures the eternal inheritance, then there is a strict connexion between Christ's sufferings and his saving benefits; but the former is true, and therefore so is the latter. Christ's death is not as a medicine laid up in a box, for such as may happen to make use of it; but it is effectually and certainly applied to all for whom it was prepared: 'By his stripes we are healed', Isa. 53:5, all that the Father hath 'given me shall come', John 6:37, saith Christ. If he obtained eternal redemption for us, then all those for whom he obtained it, do and shall enjoy that redemption; otherwise it is so far from being eternal redemption, that it is no redemption at all.

If it be said, that Christ obtained eternal redemption for all, conditionally, but not absolutely; the question is, whether Christ purchased this condition for them or not; if he did, then they must certainly enjoy it: If he did not purchase this condition, how did he obtain eternal redemption for them? Or how shall they come by this condition; as for instance, faith, seeing that it is not of a man's self, Eph. 2:8, nor is this way of enjoying this redemption, or the redemption itself, so much as revealed, and made known to multitudes of men; 'and how shall they believe in him of whom they have not heard', Rom. 10:14. Remission of sins is so great a part of redemption, that it is put for the whole of it, when it is said, 'In whom we have redemption, through his blood, the forgiveness of sins', Eph. 1:7. The latter, forgiveness of sins through Christ's blood, is here meant, by our being redeemed by his blood. If then we have the forgiveness of sins included in, or flowing from redemption by Christ's blood, then all those who were redeemed by his blood, have also forgiveness of sins, and consequently either all are pardoned, or all were not redeemed, seeing redemption necessarily includes forgiveness, or there is an inviolable connexion between them; which is the assertion I am proving. If this is disallowed, how shall we secure the honour of God's wisdom, the sincerity of his love, or maintain the value of Christ's death, or God's equity and righteousness? Was Christ's blood shed for all men, and yet are only some saved? Could Christ die at uncertainty, whether he should have a seed or no, or how great or small it should be, or whether the divine love should enjoy all, or half, or a fourth part of its objects, as it must be, if it depends on the free and uncertain will of man, whether the redeemed shall be actually saved, or not? 'God sent forth his Son, made under the law, to redeem them that were under the law, that we might receive the adoption of sons': This, in the purchase of it, we received in Christ's death, and therefore we are said to be sons, before conversion; 'Because you are sons, God has sent forth the Spirit into your hearts, crying, Abba, Father', Gal. 4:4-6. The application answers the purchase, and actually follows upon it. Christ redeemed those for whom he died from bondage, and procured for them the glorious privilege of being the sons of God; and being thus made sons, as to the price paid for it, the Father grants the thing purchased, and bestows the Spirit of adoption on the redeemed people. Now, do all enjoy this Spirit of adoption? Can all men cry, Abba, Father, or go to God with a filial frame, under the gracious influences of the Holy Spirit? If not, as is most true, then Christ did not die for all men, to redeem them from the curse, and make them sons, seeing there is such an inseparable union between redemption and adoption.

Because this argument is so conclusive and decisive, let us enter a little deeper into it, and more firmly establish it, by shewing the grounds and reasons of this strict connexion between Christ's sufferings, and his saving benefits.

(1) Christ's death had in it the nature of a *price* of redemption. We are told, in scripture, that 'we are bought with a price', 1 Cor. 6:20, and what that price was, we elsewhere read, when mention is made of the church of God, which he 'purchased with his own blood', Acts 20:28, and when it is declared that we were not 'redeemed with corruptible things, as silver and gold, but with the precious blood of Christ', 1 Pet. 1:18, 19. It is the blood of Christ, which in this business

has that use, which silver and gold has in the redeeming of captives; as one[2] has observed. It is called, in scripture, a price of redemption for the delivery of another. Now, if Christ paid a price of redemption for all, then, according to the rules of justice, all must be delivered, otherwise Christ had not his due: If then all are not delivered, Christ did not pay this price of redemption for all men, seeing all for whom he paid the price do and must enjoy the thing purchased. He who is righteous in all his ways, cannot be unrighteous to his own Son, in withholding what he had bought with his precious blood.

(2) That *love* which caused God to give his Son, and which caused Christ to give himself to redeem sinners, cannot lose or be deprived of vast numbers of persons, on whom it had fixed, and for whom it gave a ransom, and therefore all the redeemed must be saved; and if all were redeemed, then all must be saved, for God will not lose the objects of his love.

But it may be objected, the consequence drawn from the divine love doth not follow, seeing God and Christ loved all men, and intended their salvation only conditionally, provided they would believe, but left that to themselves, as being in their own power: I answer; then God and Christ left it in the power of their enemies, whether they should have any objects of their love or not; for as many never do or will believe, so the rest might not have done it, and then both Father and Son had loved in vain, and Christ had died

[2] Dr Owen against Biddle, p. 464.

in vain; and, according to the objectors, God is brought down to a mean dependence upon his creatures, unworthy of his sovereign power and grace; and God's satisfaction and honour are put into the power or subjected to the pleasure of foolish and disobedient men, Titus 3:3. But if God had such a love to all men, why did he not keep their salvation in his own hands, and secure it to them all? Could not the same love which gave Christ for all, have secured the happiness of all men, if indeed it did give him for all, and would act like itself, or according to this large extent of its objects? But, moreover, where does the scripture represent the love of God as conditional? Is it not said to be free, and from everlasting, and the spring of all the good that is wrought in or done to men? They are 'saved and called, not according to their own works, as previous conditions, but according to God's purpose and grace given them in Christ Jesus, before the world began', 2 Tim. 1:9, which is very contrary to that conditional love, mentioned in the objection.

(3) The *Father's* love to Christ renders it necessary that all such should enjoy salvation, for whom Christ, by his death, procured it. Would not a kind father, among men, certainly give to his child what he had lawfully and fully purchased? and shall not the great God give to his Son all the travail of his soul, all the purchase of his blood? Did Christ so love multitudes as to satisfy the justice of God for their sins, and obtain eternal glory for them? and shall his Father, who

loves his Son, and gives all things into his hands, John 3:35, permit his loss of a great part of the travail of his soul, and the purchase of his blood, as it actually comes to pass, if Christ loved and died for all men, and yet so great a number of them perish? How can this be consistent with the Father's love to Christ, any more than it is with Christ's love towards those for whom he died? Such a failure and loss seems to argue a great defect in the love of God to his Son, as well as a want of it to men; and carries in it an appearance of feebleness, dependence, and changeableness, no ways becoming the perfections of the great God, particularly his sovereignty, power, and infinite love, so much celebrated in scripture, and admired by the saints in all ages.

Upon the aforesaid grounds, with others that might have been mentioned, it appears, that there is a strict connexion between Christ's sufferings, and his saving benefits; or that it is reasonable to believe that all those who were reconciled to God, by the death of his Son, shall certainly be saved by his life. And from this proposition, thus established, the inference is very plain and strong, that Christ did not suffer and die to redeem all men, but a peculiar number only, who shall certainly be saved.

8. Christ died only for them for whom he purchased all the *means necessary* to their *enjoyment of salvation*; particularly faith and repentance, and the Holy Spirit, the author of each of them.

Some may wonder to hear of the purchase of the Spirit, who is a free Spirit, and works all things according to his own will; and it may be thought that he is not therefore to be bought any more than Christ was. But whatever some may think, the mission, and the work of the Holy Spirit are, in scripture, spoke of, as the fruit and effects of Christ's death; as when he said, 'Nevertheless, I tell you the truth, if I go not away, the Comforter will not come; but if I depart, I will send him to you; and, when he is come he will reprove the world of sin, of righteousness, and judgment', John 16:7, 8. By *going away* and *departing*, Christ meant his death, with what followed it: This death was necessary to the coming of the Spirit, to convince and convert sinners, and to comfort believers. The case stood thus: All men by nature, were under the law, and under the curse, in a state of sin and misery, by reason of sin: the first covenant had in it no promise, either of repentance or pardon, or of the Holy Spirit, to work the one, or apply the other, being made with a perfect man, who needed none of them; and fallen man could not receive these fruits of divine love, but by virtue of the new covenant, which was to be confirmed by the blood of Christ, which blood also purchased all the saving blessings of it, satisfied justice, removed the curse, and procured eternal life for the redeemed, and all that was previously necessary to the enjoyment of it. The church was purchased by the blood of Christ, and is made a church by the Holy Spirit, Acts 20:28, who, according to the order and method of salvation, is engaged to renew and fit for heaven all, and only those, whom Christ, by his blood, redeemed from misery, and entitled to glory. Accordingly we read, that Christ redeemed them that were under the law, by being made under the law for them, or by enduring its curse and penalty, in his death: which also procured the adoption of children for us, and the Holy Spirit to work a filial disposition in us. God sent his Son to redeem us; and, by virtue of that redemption, his Spirit, to renew us, Gal. 4:6. We receive the promise of the Spirit through faith, chapter 3:14. The ministration of the Spirit belonged not to the law, but to the gospel, which is called faith. Christ, by his accursed death, redeemed his people from the curse, and procured the promised Spirit, the attendant of the gospel dispensation, verse 13. On this account, the apostle asks, 'Received you the Spirit by the works of the law, or by hearing of faith?' Gal. 3:2. It is by virtue of the gospel covenant, ratified by the blood of Christ, that the promise of the Spirit, or the promised Spirit, is received. 'If', as one observes, 'the blood of Christ had not been shed on the cross, the Spirit had not been poured out from heaven; the effusion of the one, was the cause of the effusion of the other.' And as we obtain the Spirit, so we obtain faith through Christ, for his sake, or on account of his purchase of it. Faith is obtained through the righteousness of God our Saviour, 2 Pet. 1:1; it is on the behalf, or for the sake of Christ, that it is given to men to believe, Phil. 1:29. This gift was procured by the blood of Christ, who therefore is called 'the author and finisher of our faith', Heb. 12:2. If

Christ is the author of our faith, he must be the purchaser of it; for he gives nothing to us but what, by his merits, he purchased for us. Christ, by his death, having procured all spiritual blessings for his people, and repentance, among the rest, is exalted to give it; he is a 'Saviour to give repentance and remission of sins', Acts 5:31. These both flow from him as a Saviour, and therefore as a sufferer, as one that purchased them by his precious blood; and we are sanctified through the offering of the body of Jesus, Heb. 10:10.

It is on all hands agreed, that without faith and repentance men cannot be saved: But whence do these flow, and how do they come by them? Either men have a natural power to repent and believe, or else faith and repentance are, as the scriptures speak, the purchase and the gifts of Christ; if they are the purchase and gifts of Christ, then Christ, by his death, did not purchase salvation conditionally, if men of themselves, or by their own power, would repent and believe. He purchased salvation absolutely and perfectly, and all the necessary means of it, so as men shall repent and shall believe: and if this is true, then the conditional salvation, which, some assert, is a mere fallacy; and the redemption of all men by the death of Christ is not true, seeing all men do not receive from Christ the gifts of faith and repentance, as they should do, if he had purchased them for all men.

Our opponents,[3] indeed, deny that Christ, by his death, procured faith and repentance: in maintenance of which opinion they allege the following reasons.

---

[3] Dr Whitby on the Five Points, p. 110.

(1) They urge, that Christ wanted neither power nor will to work them in the hearts of men; to which I answer, that it might as well have been said, that Christ did not obtain eternal redemption for us, seeing he wanted neither power nor will to redeem us. The power and will of Christ, in this matter, are to be considered as acting according to the economy of, and the method of salvation agreed upon between the divine persons.[4] Christ says, that he could do nothing of himself, John 5:30, that is, beside, or beyond, or contrary to the will of the Father: now it evidently was the will of the Father, that in 'bringing many sons to glory, the Captain of our salvation should be made perfect through sufferings', and that by the effusion of his blood, he should obtain for us eternal redemption, and therefore all things included in it.

(2) It is alleged, that to make Christ procure both the promise and condition, by the same act and passion, is to turn the conditional covenant into one that is absolute; I answer, if that turn makes it conformable to God's covenant, it is so much the better. God says, 'This is the covenant that I will make; I will put my laws into their mind, and write them in their hearts; and I will be to them a God, and they shall be to me a people: All shall know me, from the least to the greatest; for I will be merciful to their unrighteousness, and their sins and iniquities will I remember no more', Heb. 8:10, 12. Let our opponents tell us, where we shall, in this account,

---

[4] 'Thou hast given him power over all flesh, that he should give eternal life to as many as thou hast given him', John 17:2.

find the condition of the covenant, on man's part. Supposing some things are required, in order to the enjoyment of other things, where is the absurdity for Christ to render the promised blessing certain, and to secure what is called the condition of enjoying it? 'Without holiness no man shall see the Lord', chapter 12:14, 'and blessed are the pure in heart, for they shall see God', Matt. 5:8. Did Christ then change the nature of the covenant, by giving himself to redeem his people from all iniquity, and to purify them unto himself?

(3) It is said, that Christ's sacrifice was not intended to procure any other benefit, but the removal of guilt. I wonder then how Paul could say, that by means of Christ's death, they who are called receive the promise of *eternal inheritance*, Heb. 9:15; is that no more than the removal of guilt? How did Christ's blood purchase the church? Did it only pay their old debt, and turn them loose to get to heaven, as well as they could of themselves?

(4) It is said, that Christ's purchase of faith and repentance is repugnant to the nature of these graces. It might as well have been said, that Christ's purchase of forgiveness is repugnant to the nature of forgiveness. If Christ has purchased the forementioned graces, then God is obliged to confer them, says the objector: and where is the harm of that? Has not God obliged himself to give Christ a seed, and that 'he shall see the travail of his soul, and shall be satisfied; and that he will

divide him a portion with the great, and that he shall divide the spoil with the strong', Isa. 53:11, 12?

How weak are these objections against our position, that Christ purchased grace, as well as eternal life, by his death. Wherein is it contrary to the nature of faith or repentance, that Christ should purchase them, seeing faith is not of a man's self, Eph. 2:8, and repentance is the gift of Christ? Why may he not purchase them, as well as give them? Is there any thing in them too great or too small for Christ to purchase? But so dark and senseless an objection, as the last above-mentioned, deserves no further notice, nor indeed that regard which has been had to it.

The objections of our opponents being thus fairly answered, our proposition stands firm and true, that Christ purchased all the necessary means of salvation, for all those for whom he died; from whence this conclusion may be drawn, that Christ did not die for all men, seeing he did not purchase the necessary means of salvation for all men.

9. The attainment of the *end* and *design* of Christ's redemption, is highly pleasing both to Christ and to his Father.

The prophet Isaiah represents God saying, 'Behold my elect in whom my soul delights', Isa. 42:1, and, by a voice from heaven, when Christ was entered upon his work, he said, 'This is my beloved Son, in whom I am well pleased', Matt. 3:17, and when Christ actually offered up himself a sacrifice to God, it is said to be of a 'sweet smelling savour', Eph. 5:2.

God was so well pleased with Christ's performance, that 'he raised him from the dead', Heb. 13:20, 'received his human nature into heaven', 1 Tim. 3:16, 'crowned it with glory and honour', Heb. 2:9, 'and placed him at his own right hand', Heb. 12:2, 'and gave him a name that is above every name', Phil. 2:9, 'appointed him a kingdom', Luke 22:29, 'and made him Lord and Judge of all', Acts 2:36, Acts 10:42, 'sent the Spirit to glorify him in the world', John 16:14, 'required all the angels of God to worship him', Heb. 1:6, 'and all men to honour the Son even as himself', John 5:23. All which things shew how satisfactory and pleasing Christ's work of redemption was to God the Father. But this satisfaction could not arise from Christ's sufferings absolutely considered; for he, who does not willingly grieve the children of men, Lam. 3:33, could not take pleasure in the sufferings of his own Son, purely on the account of the sufferings themselves; but it was with a view to the end, and the fruit of them, that they were so pleasing to him. And this naturally leads us to enquire what was the end and design of Christ's giving himself, in which God took such satisfaction: What could it be less than doing the Father's will, and finishing his work, his redeeming and saving all given him by the Father, and losing none of them, John 6:39; in a word, his glorifying the Father, and his 'bringing many sons to glory', Heb. 2:10? Christ also is represented as 'set up from everlasting, having his delights with the sons of men', Prov. 8:31: 'we perceive the love of God, in that he laid down his life for us', 1 John 3:16; 'he delighted to do this will of God', Psa. 40:8, and rejoiced in the prospect of having a body prepared for him, in which he should suffer and satisfy for the sins of men, and by dying redeem them from eternal death: This was the travail of his soul, which he was to see, and with which he was satisfied, Isa. 53:11. This was the 'joy set before him', for which he 'endured the cross', Heb. 12:2: the glory he should bring to God, and the happiness which he should procure and secure to men.

Now, if Christ redeemed men so imperfectly, and so uncertainly, as that though he died for all men, yet all men might have died eternally notwithstanding, and the most of them actually do so, what becomes of the Father's glory and man's happiness, of God's love to sinners, and Christ's strong affection to them? How could the Father be pleased in such a loose and uncertain purchase, and in so small a part of mankind, when he gave his Son to redeem all men? Could it be pleasing to him, that when he designed the redemption of all men, such a multitude should be lost, and the salvation of those who obtain it should be left so precarious, depending more on the will of man, than upon the love and care of the Father, or the redemption of the Son? With what pleasure could the all-wise God look upon such a kind of redemption as this? Or what satisfaction could Christ take in seeing the end and design of his death so greatly disappointed, if he really intended to save all men by his death, and only a remnant are saved? Or how could he be satisfied, not certainly to intend the salvation of any of those, whom he and his Father so dearly loved, and for whom he suffered such a bitter death? Could Christ be so profuse of his blood, and was his conflict with God's wrath and vengeance such a light matter, as that he could, with satisfaction, throw away the one, and endure the other, without securing the salvation of so much as one soul, instead of redeeming all men?

Upon the whole; seeing both Father and Son are so well pleased in Christ's work of redemption, and the fruit and end of it, we may conclude that Christ did not die to redeem all men conditionally and uncertainly, but that he died for a peculiar number, who shall certainly be *presented to God, with exceeding glory and joy*, Jude, verse 24, both on the part of God and Christ, and the redeemed peculiar people.

10. The redeemed are represented, in scripture, under distinct discriminating characters, or as a *select peculiar people*.

Thus they are spoke of in my text, and a multitude of other places; where they are called *Christ's people*, Matt. 1:21, *his body*, Eph. 5:23, *his sheep*, John 10:16, *the church*, Eph. 5:25, *the children of God*, John 11:52. Christ, when he said that he laid down his life for his sheep, included in that expression the elect Gentiles, those *other sheep*, chapter 10:16, which he says *he must bring*, implying, that all the chosen shall, by him, be brought to God; and he told some of the Jews, that they did not believe, because they were not of his sheep, verse 26, implying that all his sheep, for whom he laid down his life, are brought to believe in him. How could Christ be said to be the Redeemer of his people, of his body, of the church, in distinction from others, if he is the Redeemer of the whole world, of all men? The church cannot mean the world, his people cannot mean all people; those redeemed from among men, Rev. 14:4, cannot mean all men, those from among whom they were redeemed; nor can those redeemed out of every people and nation, chapter 5:9, signify all people, and all nations, or all men.

Upon this head, our opponents observe, that though Christ is said to die for his sheep, his people, and the like, yet it is not said *that he died for them only*, and none besides; but it is said that he died for the *world*, the *whole world*, or *all men*. To which I reply, that though the restrictive term, *only*, is not expressed, yet it is necessarily implied, and understood, in the scriptures, where Christ is said to die for his people, his sheep, and for his people; for if all men were intended by these expressions, what need is there of any terms of peculiarity? If all men are redeemed, then there is not a select number redeemed; for to redeem a select number out of all men, and to redeem all men, are contradictory one to the other; so that the exclusive word, *only*, is implied in those scriptures, where Christ is said to die for his sheep, and his people. It is said, 'there is one God, and one Mediator', but the word *only* is not added; shall we then say, that there are more gods than one, and more mediators than one, between God and man? When a legacy is bequeathed to one man, is it given to others, because the word *only* is not added? If when it is said, that Christ loved his church, and gave himself for it, Eph. 5:25, all men are included, because the word *only* is not added, then when men are commanded to love their wives, as Christ loved the church, they are allowed to extend their conjugal affection to all women, besides their wives, because it is not said, *Love your wives only*. This may suffice to remove the objection, and establish the proposition, that the redeemed are represented under discriminating restrictive terms; and from hence the deduction is plain, that the redeemed are a peculiar people, and not all men.

11. The *necessary means* of salvation are afforded to all those for whom Christ died, to render their salvation possible.

To deny this proposition, is to affirm that Christ died to render that possible, which, in the nature of the thing, is impossible. It is eternal life 'to know the only true God, and Jesus Christ', John 17:3. On the other hand, not to know them is eternal death. If Christ, by his death, rendered the salvation of all men possible, on the conditions of faith and repentance, it is but reasonable to suppose that they all shall enjoy the necessary means of that faith and repentance, otherwise Christ purchased a possibility of salvation, on an impossible condition, or without the necessary conditions of that possibility, or the necessary means of attaining those necessary conditions.

The dispute, at present, is not whether any man can be saved by Christ, without faith in him, but whether any man can believe in Christ, who never knows Christ, nor has heard of him; 'How shall they believe in him of whom they have not heard?' Rom. 10:14, 15. The apostle's argument lies thus: They who do not hear the word, cannot believe; they cannot hear the word, to whom it is not preached; they cannot preach it whom God doth not send: therefore they cannot be saved, to whom God does not send the preaching of the word. Thus the apostle proved the necessity of the means of grace, in order to faith, and of faith, in order to salvation. If then Christ died equally for all men, why is he not equally revealed to all men? If the greatness of men's sins did not hinder him from giving himself a ransom for all men, why should it prevent his revealing himself to all men? If infinite love moved Christ to die for all men, why did not the same love engage him to make himself known to all men? especially seeing without this knowledge they could have no faith in him, or salvation by him. Is it credible that Christ should shed his precious blood to redeem all men, and yet never discover this gracious design to them, to win their hearts, and engage them to believe in him, and adhere to him, to the saving of their souls? Did Christ die to render the salvation of all men possible, and then destroy that possibility, by withholding from thousands the necessary means of that faith, without which they could not be saved? Would this be acting like the only wise God our Saviour?

But it may be said, that the reason of God's withholding the means of grace from some, may be their obstinacy and unworthiness; the abuse of the light they had, and a foresight that they would abuse clearer light, if they had it. To this I answer, all men are naturally obstinate and unworthy; and if God deals with men according to their obstinacy and unworthiness, not only some men, but even all men should be excluded from the means of grace. If it is said, there are degrees of unworthiness, and some are better disposed than others, to improve the means, which may be a reason why they are granted to some, and withheld from others: To this it may be replied, that Christ has told us, that Tyre and Sidon, and the land of Sodom, Matt. 11:21-23, would have made a better use of his preaching than the towns of Galilee had done, yet the former never enjoyed this light, but the latter did; which plainly shews, that the means of grace are not always granted to those whom God foresaw would make a good use of them, nor are withheld from such as it was foreseen would make a bad use of them. It is best therefore to rest in that reason of this procedure assigned by Christ, God's sovereign will and pleasure; 'Thou hast hid these things from the wise and prudent, and hast revealed them to babes; even so, Father, because it seemed good in thy sight', verses 25, 26.

The general and universal terms used, concerning 'the preaching the gospel to every creature, and to all the world', Mark 16:15, 'and to the ends of the earth', Rom. 10:18, are not to be understood in the utmost extent; for so it is evident they never were, nor can be fulfilled; seeing multitudes are dead, who never heard anything of Christ or the gospel, Col.

1:23, or so much as any part of God's revealed will: 'As for his judgments, they have not known them', Psa. 147:20. For how long a time did God suffer the nations to walk in their own ways, and winked at the times of their ignorance? nay, in the days of gospel light, some places were expressly excluded from the preaching of the word: Paul and his companions being forbid by the Holy Ghost, attempted to go into Bithynia, but the Spirit suffered them not: So that the commission to 'teach all nations, and preach the word to every creature', must be explained in a general sense, and not according to the utmost extent of the words, including strictly every individual person. Not only the Jews, but the other nations were to have the light shine upon them, wherever God pleased to send his messengers: But how many are there, at this day, who know nothing of Christ, and the way of salvation by him; and is it credible that God should give his Son to be a *ransom* for all, and not give him to be a *light* to all men? Did Christ die to put all men into a salvable condition, as it is called; and then, as if he repented, leave the greatest part destitute of the necessary means of faith and salvation?

Our opponents are in the utmost distress upon this head, and know not how to reconcile an universal ransom, with a restrained and partial revelation of Christ to men. How is it consistent with the divine wisdom for Christ to die, to render the salvation of all men possible, and yet leave many of them destitute of those means, without which it is not possible, according to the scriptures, that they should be saved? 'Where there is no vision the people perish', Prov. 29:18; 'they are lost to whom the gospel is hid', 2 Cor. 4:3; 'such as have not the Son have not life', 1 John 5:12; 'without faith it is impossible to please God', Heb. 11:6; 'he that believeth not shall not see life, but the wrath of God abides upon him', John 3:36; 'and how shall men believe in him of whom they have not heard?', Rom. 10:14. So then without faith, there is no salvation; without hearing of Christ, there can be no faith in him, or salvation by him; and by withholding the revelation of Christ from vast numbers, God renders their salvation impossible, which it is said Christ, by his death, had rendered possible: And thus the purchase of the Son is made void, by the providence of the Father, according to the scheme of our opponents. But God forbid it should be so, in reality! For what kind of wisdom or prudence could there be, either in the Father, or the Son, for Christ to shed his precious blood, to redeem myriads, to whom, after all, they did not think fit to give any notice of it, or any means of enjoying the redemption obtained for them? Or, how is it consistent with the justice or goodness of God, for him to withhold the knowledge of the way of salvation from multitudes, for whom Christ purchased a possibility of salvation? Had not men better quit their notion of universal redemption, than be so injurious to the wisdom, justice, and goodness of God, as, according to their doctrine, they must unavoidably be? The difficulty is not removed by saying, that those who never enjoy the revelation of Christ, are shut out from it, by their negligence and disobedience, seeing 'Christ is found of them who sought him not, and is made manifest to them that asked not after him; and all the day long stretches out his hand to a disobedient and gain-saying people', Rom. 10:20, 21. There must then be some other reason of God's leaving so many destitute of the revelation of Christ; for this no good reason can be given, upon a supposition that Christ redeemed all men: But if it is allowed that he redeemed only a select number, good reasons may be assigned why the gospel is sent to some places, and not to others; and why it continues longer in one place, than in another, because Christ has *much people there*, Acts 18:10, and in many places it never comes, because the elect, the redeemed, obtain, but the *rest are blinded*, Rom. 11:7.

Upon the whole, our position holds true, that the necessary means of salvation are afforded to all those for whom Christ died, to render their salvation possible; and hence the conclusion follows, that Christ did not die to render the salvation of all men possible, seeing all men have not the necessary means of salvation.

12. The *intention* and *design* of Christ's redemption, is agreeable to scripture and reason, and stands clear of all absurdities and inconsistencies.

To deny this proposition, would be to cast the most injurious reflections on the Redeemer, and his work, directly contrary to God the Father; who, on the account of Christ's becoming obedient to the death of the cross, has highly exalted him, and given him a name above every name.

Christ's intention in giving himself, was, according to the scriptures, 'to redeem men from all iniquity, and purify to himself a peculiar people': and it appears to be reasonable, that his intention should be accomplished, and that he should not shed his precious blood in vain, or be disappointed of his end, with respect to the greatest part of those for whom he died. But thus it must be, if he died to render the salvation of all men possible, on condition they believe in him, and yet leaves so great a part of them under an impossibility of performing that condition, or enjoying the salvation, by not revealing or making himself known to them, as was observed before.

The scriptures nowhere speak of a conditional, uncertain redemption or men, depending on the will of the fallen creature, as to all its salutary effects. It is contrary to reason for Christ to leave salvation depending upon the will of man, which had ruined him in his best estate, and was not at all likely to save him in his worst. How could Christ expect that the intention of his death should be accomplished in such a way? Will the fallen creature take more care to secure the good effects of his death, than the Sufferer and Saviour himself did? How inconsistent and absurd must it be for Christ to exercise the greatest love towards, and inflict the greatest wrath upon the same persons, at the same time! As it must be, if he, in infinite love, died to redeem all men; and yet multitudes in hell were suffering his vengeance, at the same time he loved them, and gave himself for them. Does it not sound very harsh and shocking to say, that the saved are no more beholden to the Redeemer, than the damned? And yet this is true, if Christ loved and died equally for all men. How contrary, both to scripture and reason, is it to charge God with taking a double satisfaction for the same sins, one from Christ, and another from the damned themselves! Which yet is fact, if Christ died for all men, and satisfied the justice of God for all men. Could Christ, in infinite love, die for all men, without any fixed intention and resolution, to save any one man? Could Christ come to do the will of God, and yet subject all to the will of men, and leave it to them whether the Father should have the pleasure, and Christ the satisfaction, in redemption, foretold and promised, Isa. 53:10, 11, whether the Father should enjoy one object of his love, or Christ the travail of his soul, in one single instance or not? And yet so it was, according to their scheme, who say, that Christ died to purchase salvation conditionally for all men, but absolutely and certainly for no man, leaving to men, either to make it effectual by believing, or of no effect by their unbelief. How shall men be convinced, that Christ crucified is the wisdom of God to salvation, if not so much as one soul had its salvation certainly secured, by Christ's sufferings, and that too when, as it is said, he died to save all men?

How contrary this notion of redemption is to Christ's intention, to scripture and reason, and with how many difficulties and inconsistencies it is attended, may, in part, appear by what goes before, wherein I have not, to my knowledge, strained or misrepresented anything. But on the other hand, if God loved, and Christ died for a select number only, and effectually secured to them grace and glory; this is agreeable to scripture and reason, advances the glory of the divine perfections, and provides most for the comfort and happiness of man, as I hope to make appear, in answer to our opponents' allegations to the contrary, when I come to that part of my work.

Upon the whole, let the propositions which have been advanced, explained, and confirmed by scripture, with the plain deductions from them, be seriously and impartially considered; and then let all judge whether Christ intended to redeem all men, or some only, 'when he gave himself for us, to redeem us from all iniquity, and purify to himself a peculiar people, zealous of good works'.

Sermon 3

Titus 2:14.—Jesus Christ gave himself for us, that he might redeem us from all iniquity, and purify to himself a peculiar people, zealous of good works.

THE death of Christ being the fountain of our life, there is nothing more necessary, pleasant, or useful to the Christian, than a right apprehension and remembrance of it: And therefore there is no doctrine of the Christian religion that has been more opposed and depraved than this; some denying that Christ, strictly speaking, died for *any* man, and others as confidently affirming, that he died for *all* men, with an intention to redeem and save *all* men; whereas my text represents him as dying for a *peculiar people*. Several arguments, establishing the truth, have been insisted on, in some former discourses on this text; I now proceed to the second thing I proposed.

II. I shall *answer* the principal arguments, and vindicate the chief passages of scripture, produced in opposition to the truth which I have been defending.

1. Our opponents endeavour to prove, from the *general* and *universal* scripture terms, that Christ did not die to redeem a select number only, but *all* men. And here they produce many texts, wherein it is said, that Christ died for the *world*, the *whole* world, for *all men*, and *every man*, and the like: And it must be owned, that these words sound well on their side; and if they take them separately from the texts, and contexts, where they are used, and just in what sense they please, they may serve to make a flourish with, and may be a sufficient proof of the point, to such as look only to the surface, but not to the bottom of things, who more regard the sound, than the sense of the words, as used in the respective places: But such as understand an argument, must know, that no certain conclusion can be drawn from doubtful premises; nor can the general or universal terms prove universal redemption, till it is first proved that these terms are used in an universal sense, in the texts alleged: We deny that they are so used; and, I hope, to make it appear, that a restriction and limitation is annexed to them in the texts, or contexts, where they are used with reference to our redemption by Christ.

Before we examine particular passages, let it be observed, that they ought all to be taken in such a sense, as agrees with the express end and design of Christ's death, and never in a sense contradictory thereto. Now, the intention and design of Christ, in dying for men, is plainly expressed in the following scriptures: 'That he might sanctify and cleanse it [the church], that he might present it to himself a glorious church', Eph.

5:26, 27, 'that he might purify to himself a peculiar people', Titus 2:14, 'that he might deliver us from this present evil world', Gal. 1:4, 'that we might receive the adoption of sons', chapter 4:4, 5, 'that we might be made the righteousness of God in him', 2 Cor. 5:21, 'that he might bring us to God', 1 Pet. 3:18. It could not be the intention and design of Christ to extend redemption to such as are never purified, nor delivered from this evil world, nor receive the adoption of sons, nor are made the righteousness of God in him, nor are ever brought to God; for that would be either to have his intention disappointed, or to have intentions thwarting and contradicting one another: To suppose either of which, would be highly injurious to Christ. From hence it follows, that the largest expressions used in scripture, with relation to the extent of Christ's death, cannot be meant of all and every man, seeing Christ did not intend to sanctify every man, and bring every man to God: for if he had, he would certainly have done so; for he cannot fail in his work, nor be disappointed of his end.

(1) A great noise is made about those scriptures which speak of Christ's dying for the *world*, or the *whole* world. Accordingly a late celebrated writer, laying great stress upon the words, *the world*, and the *whole world*, tells us, that the word *world* is used almost an hundred times in St John's writings; and that the sense which the word bears therein, must be esteemed, in reason, the proper import of the word. But how, if the word is used in great variety of senses by St John? How

shall we ever the more know the proper import of it, unless we find something in the text, or context, to determine the meaning of the word, in that particular place? If the word is used almost an hundred times in St John's writings, yet I can find no more than nine places, in all his writings, in which the word *world* is applied to our redemption or salvation by Christ; and of these nine, there is not one text in which the word *world* can be proved to signify every person that has been, now is, or hereafter shall be, in this world; which is yet absolutely necessary, in order to prove, by such a text, that Christ gave himself to redeem all men, and every man. If then it can be proved, from any one verse in St John's writings, or from any other text in scripture, that the words *world*, or *whole world*, must necessarily, when applied to the work of our redemption, signify every individual man, let our opponents enjoy their conclusion, that Christ died to redeem every man: But if this cannot be done, as I am confident it cannot, why should they, from general and doubtful terms, draw an universal and certain conclusion?

I do not deny that the word *world*, is by St John, used in its utmost extent, and includes in it not only all created persons, but also all created things; as in that passage, 'The world was made by him', John 1:10. But then it does not there relate to Christ's work of redemption, but to his work of creation; and so can be no proof that Christ died to redeem all men. There are a great many places in St John's writings, and in the other parts of the New Testament, in which the word *world* is evidently used in a restrictive, limited sense. It is said of Christ, that *the world knew him not*, chapter 1:10. By the *world* here, as Chrysostom observes, is meant the multitude of sinners, addicted to worldly things: For the friends of God, those venerable men, knew Christ, even before his incarnation: The patriarch Abraham, as Christ testifies, foresaw his coming: David, in Spirit, called him *Lord*: Moses spoke of him, and all the prophets from Samuel. I may add, when he came in the flesh, some believed in him, and his 'disciples beheld his glory, and yet the world knew him not', John 1:12, 14. By *world* here every individual person cannot be meant, seeing there were many that did know Christ: But why may not these words, *The world knew him not*, as certainly prove, that no one man in the world knew Christ, as those words, 'Behold the Lamb of God, which takes away the sin of the world', chapter 1:29, signify, that Christ died for all men; especially considering, that the sin of multitudes of men is never taken away from them; the world then, from whom sin is taken, cannot mean all mankind; for by *taking away of sin*, is meant the taking it wholly away, as Chrysostom observes upon the place. When it is proved, that sin is thus taken from all men, we will allow that Christ died to redeem all men.

Christ said, 'I pray not for the world, but for those whom thou hast given me out of the world; they are not of the world, as I am not of the world', John 17:9, 16. If there is a world, which Christ does not pray for, and yet a number is given him out of that world, for whom he prays, then the word *world* cannot mean all men, both those he did pray for, and those for whom he did not pray, those who are not of the world, and those that are. If then we must judge of the import of the word *world*, by St John's writings; and if in those writings it is so often used in a restrictive sense, and never means all men, when applied to redemption, then no certain, no apparent argument can be drawn from his use of the word, for the redemption of all men, or which proves that Christ gave himself to redeem and save all men.

Christ declared, that he would give 'his flesh for the life of the world', chapter 6:51, 'and that he gives life to the world', verse 33. Seeing then Christ does not give life to all men, the world to which he giveth life, does not mean all men; therefore no good argument can be drawn from this text for universal redemption.

Christ himself has told us, that 'God so loved the world, that he gave his only begotten Son, that whosoever believeth on him, should not perish, but have everlasting life; for God sent not his Son into the world to condemn the world, but that the world, through him, might be saved: he that believes not is condemned already: He that believes on the Son, has everlasting life; and he that believes not the Son, shall not see life, but the wrath of God abides upon him', John 3:16-18, 36. Those words, 'That whosoever believeth on him should not perish, but have everlasting life', explain and limit God's love and intention, in giving his Son to save the world, and likewise serve, as a key, to let us into the meaning of the word *world*, and of all that is here spoke of it; that God, out of infinite love, gave his only begotten Son to redeem and save all men, all the world over, who, in time, believe on him; but such as never believe on him, they are condemned already, they shall not see life, but the wrath of God abides upon them: And hence it follows, that they are no part of that world which God loved, which he sent his Son to save; and consequently that world does not, cannot include in it every individual person, that ever has been, now is, or hereafter shall be in the world; for so taken, it must include those who are condemned already, those who shall not see life, those who have the wrath of God abiding upon them. This would be to charge God with pursuing two contrary ends and designs, at the same time, his condemning many, whom yet he sent his Son not to condemn, but to save; and his intention of giving life to many, concerning whom he has declared, that they shall not see life; and his loving many, upon whom his wrath always abides, who, by nature, were children of wrath, and were never delivered from that wrath. This would be to make God act as absurdly as these men argue: Not only in the verses cited, but in those that go before, Christ took care to explain the Father's intention, in sending the Son to redeem and save men, when he said; 'As Moses lifted up the serpent in the wilderness, even so must the Son of man be lifted up, that whosoever believes in him should not perish, but have everlasting life', John 3:14, 15. Here is not one word of God's love to every man, or of his intention, that his Son should redeem and save every man.

All that our opponents have to plead here, is contained in one single word, and that of a very doubtful and different signification, even the word *world*; which, in the first chapter of John, 10th verse, is evidently meant of but a part of mankind, and, for the reasons given, is so to be taken in the verses under present consideration. If our opponents deny this, and affirm, that the word *world*, is, and must be, here meant of every man, it is incumbent on them to prove their assertion, and confute our reasons to the contrary; otherwise our assertion, that it means only *some* men, not *all* men, is as good a proof of our doctrine of particular redemption, as their bare assertion that the word *world* means all men, can be that Christ died to redeem all men. But we will be so generous, as to give up the cause to them, if they can fairly, not from this chapter only, but from any other scripture, make it appear that the word *world*, applied to our redemption and salvation by Christ, does, and must, evidently mean all mankind, without exception. And if they cannot, how vain are all their flourishes, and how impotent is all their declamation upon this word! Till this is done, they ought not to give themselves, or others, so much trouble about an ambiguous word, which is used in so many different senses in scripture.

It may be said, if the word *world* cannot be proved to signify all men, in any place relating to redemption, yet in all such places it includes the wicked and ungodly, as well as the good, and therefore it is equivalent to an universal; for if Christ died for the evil and for the good, he died for all men, seeing the whole species, or kind, is comprehended in this subdivision. To this I answer in general, God justifies the ungodly, and he justifies the godly; and therefore according to this way of arguing, he justifies all men, which is both false and absurd to suppose; But, to be more particular, it is not true, that the word *world*, in all those places relating to redemption, includes the finally wicked and ungodly.

It is indeed boldly asserted, that the word *world* never signifies the elect only, in opposition to the wicked of the world; but still the wicked of the world, in opposition to the faithful Christians. We do not deny that Christ 'died for the ungodly; that when we were enemies, we were reconciled to God, by the death of his Son'; nor can it be denied that Christ died for his sheep, for his church, for believers; but then we are to know that the ungodly man, and the enemy, for whom Christ died, is the same with the good man, the reconciled, the sheep, the believer: These different or contrary denominations point out not two different sorts of men, those who are saved, and those that perish; but two different states of the same persons, what they are by nature, and what they are by grace; what they were before conversion, enemies, wicked, and ungodly; and what they are at and after conversion, reconciled, believers, faithful, the church, and Christ's sheep.

There are several places, relating to our redemption by Christ, where the word *world* is to be understood of the elect, or believers only: As 'God sent his Son into the world, that, through him, the world might be saved', John 3:17, but only believers are saved through Christ; believers therefore are that world which Christ was sent to save: 'Christ gives life to the world', John 6:33, but Christ gives life only to believers; and therefore believers only are that world, to which Christ gives life. 'God was in Christ reconciling the world to himself, not imputing their trespasses unto them', 2 Cor. 5:19. But the world, to whom God does not impute their trespasses, are only believers; therefore only believers are meant by that world, which God was in Christ reconciling to himself. This last cited text does not barely exhibit to us the form of doctrine, which the ministers of reconciliation were to preach, but the matter of fact already done; God had been atoned, by the sacrifice offered by his Son, for that world, to whom he does not impute their trespasses, but who are made the righteousness of God in him: Hence it is said, '*he was*, not *he will be*, reconciling the world to himself'. And the apostle first asserts, that the reconciliation was made by Christ, and then tells us, that the ministry of this reconciliation was committed to him and his brethren.

Augustine, in his dispute with the Donatists, explains the last cited scripture, as we have done: 'They [the Donatists] will not consent [says he] that the church can be signified by the word *world*, contrary to the words of the apostle, "God was in Christ, reconciling the world to himself"; and contrary to the words of our Lord himself, who saith, "The Son of man came not to judge the world, but that the world might be saved by him"; for the world could neither be reconciled to

God, nor saved by him, unless by the word *world* the church be understood, which only being reconciled to God, shall be saved by him.'

The apostle tells the Colossians, that 'the gospel was come into *all the world*, and brought forth fruit', Col. 1:6. What can here be meant by *all the world*, but believers? For in others the gospel does not bring forth fruit, as it did in the Colossians. Other places might be produced, in which the word *world* is to be understood of the elect or believers only; but I cannot find one place in which the word *world*, when used with relation to redemption, signifies those that perish, and much less such only.—In answer to the objection, let it be observed farther, that supposing the whole *world* always meant the wicked and ungodly, yet it cannot be proved that it means all the wicked, and all the ungodly, those who perish, as well as those who are saved; and consequently this mighty word *world* affords no solid argument for universal redemption. It is very remarkable, that though God is said to *love the world*, yet it is nowhere said, in scripture, that he loves all men: and though Christ is said to *give his flesh for the life of the world*, yet it is nowhere said that he gave his flesh for the life of all men, or of all mankind.

If the word *world* will not make out the point, our opponents think that universal redemption is fully proved by these words: 'He is the propitiation for our sins, and not for ours only, but for the sins of the whole world', 1 John 2:2. It is not said, he is the propitiation for our sins, and for the sins of every man, or of all mankind besides: that would have made the proof clear and decisive. But, before I come to the particular answer to this allegation, let it be observed in general, that those words in the text, *the whole world*, are evidently used in a limited restrictive sense: As the antithesis shews, 'and not for ours only, but for the sins of the whole world'; so that there is a whole world besides those meant by the apostle, when he says, 'He is the propitiation for our sins', his own, and those to whom he wrote. Our opponents therefore stumble at the threshold, and produce a text, which, at first sight, shews, that those big-sounding words, *the whole world*, do not, even in that place, signify all and every in the world, but a part of it, distinguished from the rest, as has been already noted.

It is said, that the words, *the whole world*, never, in scripture, signify the elect only, in opposition to the wicked, in the whole world: To which I reply, that the words, *all the world*, which are equivalent to *the whole world*, are evidently used concerning the elect. 'The gospel was come into all the world, and brought forth fruit', Col. 1:6. All the world in whom the gospel brought forth fruit, must here mean the elect, believers; for in others it did not bring forth fruit. The apostle John said, 'We are of God, and the whole world lieth in wickedness', 1 John 5:19. The whole world here evidently signifies the worse and wicked part of the world; and when it is said, 'He is the propitiation for the sins of the whole world', why may not the words denote the better part of the world, the elect, the church of God? We have as good a right, and greater reason, to affirm it, than others have to deny it.

[1] The word *propitiation* seems to limit the expression to believers: 'God has set forth his Son to be a propitiation, through faith in his blood.' The word *propitiation*, in scripture, never extends to any but believers, or refers to any others; so vain is the attempt to apply it to all mankind, and thereby prove universal redemption.

[2] The persons for whom Christ is said to be a propitiation, are those for whom he is an advocate, or intercessor; but he is not an intercessor for all men, and therefore he was not a propitiation for the sins of all men; and consequently the apostle could not mean every individual man when he said, that 'Christ was a propitiation for the sins of the whole world'. There is an inseparable connexion between the propitiation and the intercession: 'We have an advocate with the Father, Jesus Christ the righteous, who also is the propitiation for our sins, yea for the sins of the whole world'; for the sins of all for whom he is an advocate with the Father; for his intercession is founded upon his sacrifice: he suffered and satisfied for those for whom he intercedes; and therefore his intercession is effectual, or prevalent with God. This seems to be the sum and scope of the apostle's reasoning; and it very clearly points out whom he intends by the whole world, for whose sins Christ is said to be a propitiation.

[3] The scope of the apostle is to comfort weak believers, under an over-bearing sense of their sinful infirmities. The argument he uses is, Christ's pleading in heaven the virtue of that atoning sacrifice, which he had offered on earth, not only for their particular sins, but for the sins of all his people throughout the world: And a sacrifice of such virtue and extent, he intimates, would bear a sufficient plea for the remission of their sins. According to our doctrine, the apostle's reasoning is just, and the consolation strong: But what comfort can it be to a poor dejected Christian, oppressed with his guilty fears, to tell him, that Christ loved and died for all men alike; for Cain and Judas, as well as for any others; that there was a possibility of pardon and life procured for all, if they would believe and repent; this they must do of themselves, and when they have done it, they may fall from their faith into eternal perdition; and that this universal propitiation has neither purchased grace for unbelievers, nor perseverance for true believers, but left it to themselves, to believe and repent, and mortify sin, and secure eternal life by their own power? Is this the doctrine of the gospel? Is this strong consolation? May not the poor distressed soul say, Miserable comforters are ye all? 'But God has, by two immutable things, in which it is impossible for him to lie, given strong, and much better consolation to the heirs of promise, who have fled for refuge to Christ, and have laid hold on the hope set before them', Heb. 6:18.

[4] The words, *the whole world*, are in scripture generally, if not always, used in a restrictive sense. A decree was made, that *the whole world should be taxed*, which whole world was no more than the whole Roman empire, Luke 2:1. The devil is said to *deceive the whole world*, Rev. 12:9, and yet it was impossible that he should deceive the elect: Christ said to the church in Philadelphia, 'I will keep thee from the hour of temptation, which shall come upon the whole world', chapter 3:10. The apostle Paul said to the believers at Rome, 'Your faith is spoke of throughout the whole world', Rom. 1:8, and yet a great part of the world were dead before they believed. If then the whole world generally signifies but part of mankind, we demand a reason why it must mean every man, in the text under consideration.

[5] The apostle John was a minister of the circumcision: At first he preached only to the Jews: they would allow the Gentiles, whom they called *the world*, no part with them in the great salvation: and it appears to have been a distinction much in use, at first, between Jew and Gentile; the former were called God's people; the latter the world. Hence the falling of the Jews is said to be *the riches of the world*, or the Gentiles, Rom. 11:12. Accordingly St John might, by *the world*, signify the Gentiles; and teach us, that all believers, among all nations, and not only among the Jews, had the benefit and comfort of Christ's sacrifice and intercession.

[6] It being agreed between us, that the apostle's scope and design is to comfort believers, dejected with a sense of their sins, the question is, which tends most to comfort them, the asserting that Christ procured a possible or conditional reconciliation for all men, or a certain and eternal redemption for a select and chosen number? to bring this debate to a short issue; when our opponents have spent their whole strength in asserting, and as they think, proving, that Christ was the propitiation for the sins of all mankind, without exception, yet, at last, they are forced to own, that none but final believers shall obtain eternal life; and we constantly affirm, with the scripture, that all who believe in Christ shall be saved: Wherein, then, is their doctrine more comfortable than ours, or indeed so much? The comfort belongs only to believers, and to all such, whether Christ died to redeem all men, or some only: But those who hold the latter say, not only that such *may*, but that they *shall* believe. All that the Father has given Christ, shall come, and such as come, shall not be rejected, or fall from their faith and happiness, John 6:37, for 'Christ's sheep hear his voice, and follow him, and he gives them eternal life, and they shall never perish', chapter 10:28.—On these accounts, and on others, that might have been added, we maintain, that there was no need to assert, that Christ is the propitiation for the sins of every man conditionally, in order to believers' comfort, seeing without that assertion their comfort is more effectually and sufficiently provided for: And, from all the forementioned reasons put

together, we conclude, that God's chosen throughout the world, are the persons for whose sins Christ was a propitiation.

Upon the whole, the scripture, when it speaks of the world of the redeemed, represents them by universal terms, but yet so as to mean the elect only. Which Prosper elegantly expresses: 'In the elect and foreknown, and from all generality severed, a certain, special universality is supposed; so as the whole world is freed out of the whole world, and all men seem to be redeemed from among all men.' 'Now also Christ was subject to the Father, yet not for all, but for believers in him only, for whom he offered himself to the Father, as the immaculate Lamb, that he might present us to his Father, freed from all sin', as Cyril of Alexandria expresses it. This was the sense of leading men in the church of God, after this point had been more attentively looked into and examined. Concerning which, some of the ancients had expressed themselves with less care, before it came to be the subject of more close debate.

(2) Our opponents insist much on several other general or universal terms used in scripture, which, as they think, prove universal redemption; or that Christ gave himself to redeem all and every individual man. Here they urge the words *all*, *all men*, *every man*, with as much vehemence, and to as little purpose, as they had pleaded the words *world*, and *whole world*, in favour of their opinion. That they may not think

themselves neglected, I shall cite the principal texts produced, with some short remarks.

Before I enter upon the particular instances, let it be observed, that the word *all*, in many places, some say near five hundred, is used with limitation, and does not signify every individual person, or thing. Thus it is said, that 'Christ healed all that were sick', Matt. 8:16, not all men who lived and died before he came in the flesh, or who lived at that time, but all that came or were brought to him. So Paul said, that 'he pleased all men in all things', 1 Cor. 10:33, whereas he knew but a part of the world, and pleased but some of these he did know, and of them but few, if any, in all things. He also said, 'All things are lawful to me', verse 23. What a horrid assertion would this be, strictly taken! God promised to 'pour out his Spirit on all flesh', Acts 2:17, not every individual person, but upon some of all sorts, ages, and degrees. Prayers are to be made for *all men*, 1 Tim. 2:16, but not for the dead and damned, or those that have sinned to death, 1 John 5:16. So, with relation to the resurrection, it is said, 'In Christ shall all be made alive', 1 Cor 15:22, but not strictly every man, for a great number shall not die, and therefore cannot rise again, verse 51. It shews a strong bias to an opinion for our adversaries to bring this text to prove universal redemption, which, when they have tortured it all they can, will never so much as prove an universal resurrection. The same may be said as to other texts they produce; however, let their allegations from scripture have a fair hearing.

[1] Our Lord Jesus Christ said; 'I, if I am lifted up from the earth, will draw all men to me', John 12:32. Now, say some, he who, by his death, draws *all men to him*, undoubtedly *died for all men*. But this text is ill chose as a witness for universal redemption, seeing Christ could not mean all men, and every man, by the *all* that he would draw to him; for he told the unbelieving Jews that they *would not come to him*, chapter 5:40, and at the very time when Christ spoke these words, there were multitudes in the prison of hell, who could never be drawn to him in any sense. A noted writer, on the other side, interprets the cited text of Christ's engaging many, throughout all the parts of the world, to believe in him: But how is that a proof of universal redemption? Chrysostom, by *all*, understands the Gentiles; and by Christ's *drawing*, understands his bringing men to believe. Now, if it can be proved that Christ brings all men to believe on him, we shall readily allow, that he died, or was lifted up, to redeem all men.

[2] It is said by the apostle Paul, that 'God has concluded them all in unbelief, that he might have mercy on all', Rom. 11:32. By *all*, Jews and Gentiles are here meant; not as a strict universality: for so taken, God has not mercy, saving mercy on all, but upon some of them only. There is *severity* exercised towards the unbelieving Jews, verse 22, and the apostle's highest aim was to save *some* of them, verse 14, which makes it very plain, that not all the Jews, much less all men, strictly taken, are meant by the *all*, which the scripture says God would have mercy upon.

[3.] Our opponents urge that scripture, 'As by the offence of one, judgment came upon all men to condemnation; so by the righteousness of one, the free gift came upon all men to justification of life', Rom. 5:18. It is observed, 'that the apostle is comparing the condemnation, which was procured by the sin of the first Adam, with the free gift of justification, procured by the second Adam, as to the extent of persons concerned in both'. Be it so; Adam brought condemnation and death upon all his seed; so Christ brought justification and eternal life upon all his seed: All men, in the ordinary course of generation, are the seed of the first Adam; but all men, so taken, are not the seed of the second Adam; for the redeemed are a 'peculiar people, selected out of every kindred, and tongue, and people, and nation', Rev. 5:9. And yet they may be said to be all men, in a federal sense, or all men given him by the Father, or all who, in time, believe on him. Thus the apostle himself states the comparison, in these words; 'As in Adam all die, so in Christ shall all be made alive. But every man in his own order; Christ the first fruits, afterwards they that are Christ's at his coming', 1 Cor. 15:22, 23. It appears, from hence, that death by the first Adam, and life by the second Adam, follow union with either of them; all in the first Adam sinned, and die in and with him; all in Christ, the second Adam, who are said to be his, in distinction from others who are not his, shall be made alive, shall rise, and live with him for ever. There is, then, an *all*, which is restrained to them that are Christ's; but such a distinction, or limitation, had been not only impertinent, but false, if all men were in him, or if justification of life was procured for, and offered to all men by Christ, as our adversaries explain it. In a few words, we readily allow, that Christ died to redeem all those men upon whom the free gift comes to justification of life, in the same sense, as by Adam's offence judgment came upon all men to condemnation; that is, if all men are actually justified by Christ, and have the sentence of eternal life to pass upon them, then we must allow that Christ died to redeem and save all men; and till that be proved, the scripture in debate between us will be of little service to the cause of universal redemption. To say that the same *all* that died, and were condemned, in and with the first Adam, are justified, and live in and with the second Adam, is to beg the question, and to leave the devils no company in hell.

[4] Another text pleaded in favour of universal redemption is this: 'if one died for all, then were all dead; and that he died for all, that they which live, should not henceforth live to themselves, but to him that died for them, and rose again', 2 Cor. 5:14, 15. Our opponents argue, from this text, that those words, *all were dead*, must certainly be taken in their greatest latitude, wherefore the words preceding, *Christ died for all*, from which they are an inference, ought also to be taken in the same extent. Now, to clear the sense of the text, let us consider,

(i) The apostle's scope and design is to shew how we are constrained and obliged to live to Christ, and not to ourselves;

and therefore every passage is to be interpreted so as may best agree with his design. Now, if we understand these words, *all were dead*, of a being dead in sin; what argument do they afford for our *living to Christ*? All were dead in sin, therefore we are bound to live to Christ; where is the force of the reasoning? But if we interpret the words not of a being dead *in* sin, but of our being dead *to* sin, as it is elsewhere explained,[1] then the reason is strong; but the argument for universal redemption is lost: for all men are not dead to sin; and if those who are, or shall be so dead, are the *all* for whom Christ died; then by that *all*, all mankind cannot be intended. Even some of the other side themselves, by 'the all that were dead', understand not all who were dead in sin, but all who are dead to sin, by virtue of Christ's death: *All ought to die*, namely, to sin. The sense is the same with that in the beginning of the sixth chapter of the epistle to the Romans, though more briefly expressed. According to the apostle he understands all Christians, in whom the efficacy of the death of Christ exerts itself; so far as they, by the example of Christ, are 'dead to sin and the flesh', says another upon those words, *Then were all dead*.

(ii) The extent of the *all* who were dead, is to be taken from the *all* Christ died for. The apostle affirms so many to be dead as Christ died for; not that Christ died for so many

---

[1] 'Our old man is crucified with him, that the body of sin might be destroyed, that henceforth we should not serve sin', Rom. 6:6. 'Who his own self bore our sins in his own body upon the tree, that we being dead to sin, should live unto righteousness', 1 Pet. 2:24.

as were dead. If *one died for all*, for all whom he loved, and
for whom he rose again, then all those persons were dead,
they died with Christ; the old man was crucified with him:
they, by Christ's cross, became dead to sin, that they might
no longer live therein. But is this the effect of the death of
Christ upon all men, or upon some only? Let this determine
who the *all men* are, for whom Christ died.

It may be objected, that there seems to be a manifest
distinction between the *all* whom Christ died for and who
were dead, and those who, by virtue of Christ's death, live;
whereas if being dead to sin was the thing intended, then if
it is not the same thing, yet it would belong to all the same
persons, and at the same time to be dead, and to live; for
the death of sin, and the life of grace, are of the same date,
or commence at the same time, and extend to all the same
persons: The words in the text lie thus: 'And that he died for
all, that henceforth they that live', implying, that all those
do not live for whom Christ died, but that such of them as
do live, are bound to live to Christ, and not to themselves.
I must say, that the objection is set in a strong light, and, at
first sight, carries in it something very plausible and engaging; but yet I hope to make it appear not to be the sense of
the text. The apostle here, as he often does elsewhere,[2] and as
we commonly do, uses an elliptical sort of speech, as appears

---

[2] 'What the law could not do, in that it was weak through our flesh, God sending his own Son in the likeness of sinful flesh [he did] that the righteousness', etc.
Rom. 8:3. So chapter 5:18: 'As by the offence of one [*judgment came*] upon all men
to condemnation.'

from that passage, *And that he died for all.* To make which clear and full, we must add those words, 'We thus judge, that he died for all, that henceforth they that live should not live to themselves'; where is understood that the *all* who were dead to sin, by the cross of Christ, at the same time received a principle of spiritual life, which was to be improved in living to Christ; so that by *all that were dead*, and *those that live*, the apostle means the same persons, though he does not take up time to say, we thus judge, that all died to sin in Christ; and all, at the same time, live in him by faith; and, from that very moment, are bound to live to Christ in newness of life. It was taken for granted, by the apostle, that men could not be dead to sin, but, at the same time, they must live in Christ; 'for without him we can do nothing', John 15:5, and therefore, without explaining all this, he describes the same persons, who were, in one sense, dead; to be, in another sense, alive; and bound to use that life, in obeying and glorifying Christ: The word *henceforth* favours this sense; 'Then were all dead, that henceforth they who live, should not live to themselves, but to Christ.' What kind of reasoning would it be to say, that Christ died for all that were dead in sins, that henceforth among all that were dead in sins, those who live, should not live to themselves: But to say all were dead to sin, by the death of Christ, that henceforth, or from that very time, they should not live to themselves, but to Christ, who died for them, and rose again, is good and strong reasoning, and of a gospel strain. I think, the argument runs clear and strong, if we apprehend the apostle thus speaking: 'In persuading men to fly from the wrath to come, and receive Christ, we feel the constraining influences of his love, in dying for his people, and engaging them all to die to sin, and live to himself.' If this is the genuine sense of the text, as I take it to be, the force of the objection is taken off at once; and, I hope, more need not be said in answer to it.

(iii) The *all* for whom Christ is said to *die* are those very persons for whose justification he rose again, Rom. 4:25. I ask then, did Christ rise again for the justification of all then? If not, then all mankind are not meant by the *all* for whom Christ died.

(iv) The *all* for whom Christ died, are *new creatures*, 2 Cor. 5:17. Their sins are not *imputed* to them, and they are actually *reconciled* to God, verse 19, and they are made the righteousness of God in Christ, verse 21. But this is not the case of all men in the world, but of all the elect, all believers; and hence it follows, that the *all* for whom Christ died, are not all men that ever were, are, or shall be; and consequently that from this text it cannot be proved that Christ died for all mankind.

[5] Another text alleged in favour of universal redemption, is this which follows: 'Who will have all men to be saved, and come to the knowledge of the truth; who gave himself a ransom for all, to be testified in due time', 1 Tim. 2:4, 6. Our opponents think the cited words to be a clear declaration of the intention both of the Father and of the Son, relating to

man's redemption; of the Father it is said, that he would have 'all men to be saved'; and concerning the Son, that he 'gave himself a ransom for all'; and hence they conclude, that *Christ died for all and every man*. In vindication of this scripture, and in answer to the argument drawn from it, let it be observed,

(i) That the whole force of the argument depends upon the sense of the word *all*, which, in the very context, is used in a limited and restrained sense, and can never be proved to be used in its largest sense, in the text under consideration. A little before it is said, that 'supplications and prayers are to be made for all men, for kings, and for all in authority', verse 1; now, are we here, by *all men*, to understand *every man*? Are Christians to pray for the dead, as well as the living; for the damned in hell, or the glorified in heaven; for those unborn and unknown? In the same place it is said, that *thanks* are to be made to God for all men; what! for Judas, Cain, and Antichrist, and all who are suffering the vengeance of eternal fire? If *all men* to be prayed for, and for whom thanks are to be given, mean only *some men* of *all ranks* and *nations*, especially those who have it in their power to do more good or harm than others, as public magistrates, and the like; then by the *all men*, whom God would have to be saved, and for whom Christ is a ransom, may be meant only some men, some of all sorts, ranks, and conditions, which are to be prayed for, seeing God has now enlarged the pale of the church, the Gentiles flowing into it. The will of God that *men should come to the knowledge of the truth*, and that *they should be saved*, is equally extensive; for they are joined together, without any the least distinction, or sign of difference between them. 'God will have all men to be saved, and come to the knowledge of the truth': All then to whom God does not grant the means of coming to the knowledge of the truth, are excluded from the all, whom God will have to be saved, and for whom Christ gave himself a ransom.

(ii) The *will of God* here must mean either God's significa-tion of what he requires men to do, or a declaration of what he himself will certainly do. Wherever God's word comes, he requires all men to repent; but the event shews that he does not give repentance to all men, or work it in them.[3] He commanded Pharaoh to *let Israel go*, and yet foretold that he would *harden Pharaoh's heart*, so as he should not hearken, Exod. 7:2-4, where there is a very plain distinction between God's secret and his revealed will, between what he calls man to do, and what he will do himself. The same appears in the case of Abraham's offering up his son Isaac, and in many others. When, in the text under consideration, it is said, that *God will have all men to be saved*, the meaning may be, that he requires all men, to whom he sends his word, to *seek salvation*. Some observe, that it is not said that *God will save all men*, as expressing the certainty of what he will do; but

---

[3] 'As I live, saith the Lord God, I have no pleasure in the death of the wicked, but that the wicked turn from his way and live', Ezek. 33:11. It doth not hence follow, that God would have all men, even the wicked saved, but only that he takes pleasure in the conversion and salvation of the wicked, as the last clause explains it: but that 'the wicked turn from his way and live'.

he will have all men to be saved, as expressing the duty of all men to seek salvation. If by the *will of God* is meant in the text the good pleasure of his will, or the good pleasure which he hath purposed in himself, Eph. 1:5, 9, then all mankind cannot be meant, by the *all* whom God will have to be saved, and come to the knowledge of the truth; seeing God 'works all things according to the counsel of his own will', verse 11, but God does not actually save all men; yet 'his counsel shall stand', Isa. 46:10, 'and he will do all his pleasure, in the host of heaven, and among the inhabitants of the earth', Dan. 4:35; 'who has resisted his will, or who can do it?' Rom. 9:19. Now, this is the will of God, 'that of all whom he gave to Christ, he should lose nothing, but should raise it up at the last day', John 6:39. If then it was the will of God that all mankind should be saved, all mankind would actually be saved; and if all are not actually saved from sin and wrath, then the text in debate cannot mean that God will have every individual person to be saved, and consequently that Christ's giving himself a ransom for all, cannot mean all mankind, but the *all* given him by the Father; for, as he said, 'he came down from heaven to do the will of him that sent him', verses 38, 39.

It may be said, God willed the salvation of all men conditionally, or if they will be saved. To this I answer: for God to will the salvation of all men, if they will, is not to will it at all; for all men might have rejected. Nothing can be affirmed certainly of such a will of God, as depends upon the uncertain will of the creature. If all men will be saved, then God wills the salvation of all men; if no man will be saved, then God wills the salvation of no man: He has no will of his own who must be determined by the will of another, and that other is not determined by his will. This notion represents God as saying, I will that every individual person should be saved; nevertheless, not as I will, but as they will. Is not this to make the will of God, mutable and uncertain? And, on this supposition, what becomes of the immutability of his counsel, Heb. 6:17, or how 'does he work all things according to the counsel of his own will', Eph. 1:11. Is not this evidently to dethrone God, and set up man in his room?

(iii) The will of God, that all men should be saved, is commensurate to his will, that 'all men should come to the knowledge of the truth': but it is not his will that all men should come to the knowledge of the truth; for to some he does not give a capacity to know it, as idiots, madmen: and to others, he does not give, yea, he actually withholds, the means 'of coming to the knowledge of the truth', Psa. 147:19, 20; Acts 16:6, 7; 17:30, and some he 'gives over to strong delusions, to believe a lie, that they may be damned', 2 Thess. 2:11, 12, therefore he does not will that all men should come to the knowledge of the truth, or that all mankind should be saved.

It gives us a very ill representation of God to say, that he willed the salvation of all men if they will, when he well knew that multitudes never would choose or desire salvation from sin and wrath, and that he never would make them willing, by his own gracious power; for this is trifling with men, in a matter of the highest importance, and a pretending that love towards them, which had no reality in it, and could be no more than a delusive shew and appearance of it.—From what has been said, I think, it may clearly appear, that the scripture which has been so largely considered, does not prove that Christ died to redeem and save all men.

[6] It is urged, that Christ 'tasted death for every man', Heb. 2:9, and our opponents make a mighty flourish with this text, and would have us believe that it concludes clearly and strongly on their side. In answer to this, let it be considered, that the word *man* is not in the Greek text, though if it had, it would have given little or no strength to their argument; for, in reason, it must have been explained agreeably to the context, 'Christ tasted death for all men', 'or every man, who is one of the many sons to be brought to glory', Heb. 2:10, and of whose salvation he is the captain: every man that is his brother, and is sanctified by him, verse 11, every man who is one of the children whom God had given him, verse 13, every man who, by his death, is delivered from eternal death, every man that is reconciled by his death, verse 17,. But this is not the lot of all men in the world; and therefore when it is said, that 'Christ tasted death for every man', the apostle does not mean that he died to redeem and save all mankind.

It may be said, though the words *world, whole world,* and *all,* may admit of a restriction, and not always signify all mankind, yet the words *every man,* seem so very full and express, that there is no room to evade the force of this testimony for universal redemption. To which I reply, that these very words, *every man*, are elsewhere used in a restrictive and limited sense; and therefore may be so in the cited scripture. The apostle says, 'Warning every man, and teaching every man', Col. 1:28. 'The manifestation of the Spirit is given to every man, to profit with', 1 Cor. 12:7. Nay, Christ said, 'Go preach the gospel to every creature', Mark 16:15. Not to birds or beasts, or every man that has been, then was, or should be, upon the face of the earth; but generally and without distinction, as to nation or rank, to as many as they could, wherever they came. No argument, therefore, can be drawn, for the uncertain meaning of the words, *every man*, as signifying every man that ever was, now is, or hereafter shall be, seeing they are so often taken in a limited sense; and, according to the context, are so to be understood, in the scripture alleged.

[7] Another text produced in favour of universal redemption, is the following: 'He is the Saviour of all men, especially of those who believe', 1 Tim. 4:10. According to our opponents, Christ is the Saviour of all men, as to impetration or purchase; and the Saviour of believers, as to their actual possession and enjoyment of salvation. But here are several things to be proved before this text will establish the doctrine of universal redemption, which, I believe, will never be done.

(i) It should be demonstrated, that the Saviour here spoke of is Jesus Christ: There is not a syllable in the text to cause us to think so. The Saviour here spoke of is said to be the living God, a title not appropriated to Christ, though he is not excluded from it, but is, on other occasions, so called: and it may be used of God indefinitely, who is 'the Hope of Israel; and the Saviour thereof in times of trouble', Jer. 14:8.

(ii) It should be proved, that the salvation here signified is spiritual and *eternal* salvation; whereas, to an impartial judge, it must rather appear to be meant of a *temporal* and *providential* salvation: The context, I think, carries it evidently this way, if we read the words in their connexion: 'Therefore we both labour and suffer reproach, because we trust in the living God, who is the Saviour of all men, especially of those that believe': or we trust in the living God for support and preservation, in the labours, and under the reproaches, which our preaching the gospel occasions; and we have this trust in God, because he is the Preserver of all men, and especially of his own people; for godliness has the promise of this life, and also of that to come; and therefore he will preserve us here, so far as he sees fit: And it is to be remembered, that Paul had a particular intimation of this, when he first received his commission from Christ, who said, 'I will appear to thee, delivering thee from the people and the Gentiles, to whom now I send thee', Acts 26:17. Now, what relation has this to universal redemption? I have often wondered, how men of ingenuity and learning could lay such a stress upon this text, which is nothing to their purpose, even allowing, though I will only suppose, the opinion of some of the ancient writers to be true, that the word *Saviour* means *Preserver*, as it refers to all men; and *eternal* salvation, as it refers to believers; for even in that way it makes nothing for universal redemption. It is said, that Chrysostom, Œcumenius, Primasius, and Ambrose, came into this last interpretation; so did Thomas Aquinas, and others; but I must freely own, that the former explanation of the text seems more solid, pertinent, and evidently just and true.

(iii) Before this text can establish universal redemption, it must be proved, that there is an actual universal salvation: for the text does not say that God *may be*, by virtue of certain remote conditions and possibilities, the Saviour of all men; but, in that sense in which he is the Saviour of all men, he actually *is so* at present. Now, if it can be proved, that all mankind are actually saved from sin, death, and hell, the dispute is at an end at once; and with what joy shall we come over to the tenets of our opponents!

(iv) I cannot see how they will be able to draw a possible conditional salvation out of those words, 'especially of those that believe'; and as to the other part of the verse, there is nothing that looks like it. Upon the whole I conclude, that the text yields no support to the doctrine of universal redemption. Our opponents have other arguments, from reason, to offer, and some objections against our doctrine to make; the consideration of which will be the subject of my next and last discourse.

Sermon 4

Titus 2:14.—Jesus Christ gave himself for us, that he might redeem us from all iniquity, and purify to himself a peculiar people, zealous of good works.

HAVING, in some former discourses, offered several arguments in defence of the doctrine of particular redemption, in my last on this subject I made an entrance upon the consideration of the arguments produced by our opponents, in favour of the notion of Christ's dying for all men; and I went through the objection against our doctrine, which is built on the general terms used in scripture; such as the *world*, the *whole world*, all men, and *every man*. I shall now examine some other objections, which are made to our opinion. Therefore,

2. I shall proceed to another set of objections, which are brought against the doctrine of particular redemption, and which the enemies of it have always in their mouths, and make a great noise with. They pretend that the opinion of Christ's dying for a certain determinate number, is inconsistent with

the general calls which are given in scripture, to all men, to believe and repent, that it detracts from the goodness and grace of God, and from the merit of Christ; that it represents God as partial or unjust to his creatures, and that it takes away all comfort from poor sinners. These things sound plausibly; but if the objections are severally and distinctly examined they will appear to be of no weight.

(1) The patrons of universal redemption often tell us, that all men are, in scripture, called to *repent* and *believe*; therefore Christ died to redeem all men. It is pleaded, John 1:7, that John the Baptist came to bear witness to Christ, that all men through him might believe; that the apostles, Mark 16:15, 16, were to 'go into all the world, and preach the gospel to every creature'; and every individual that would believe, and be baptized, was to be saved; that 'the Holy Spirit was to come and convince the world of sin, because they believed not in Christ', John 16:8, and that the apostle Paul, Acts 17:30, in his speech to the Athenians, declared that 'God commanded all men every where to repent'.

These allegations may be thought to have a great deal in them by such as are taken with the bare sound of words, without considering their meaning; but it is a sufficient answer if we say, that seeing multitudes in the world have not enjoyed the scriptures, nor the preaching of the gospel, it is evident that all men, strictly and absolutely speaking, have not been called to believe and repent. All the men to whom the ministry of John the Baptist extended, were far from being all men in the world; for there were multitudes dead before he was born, multitudes in his time who never heard him, and multitudes since who never knew anything of his witness or testimony: therefore all the men that might or should be influenced by his ministry to believe, could not be meant of all the individual men in the world. The apostles 'going into all the world, and preaching the gospel to every creature', must not be interpreted of all the individuals of mankind, in their day, much less of all the sons and daughters of Adam; for then they neither did nor could fulfil their commission: And the next branch of the cited scripture, 'He that believes shall be saved', is rather an epitome of the gospel, which they were to preach, wherever they came, than a command to all men to believe: Besides, we may understand the words, as declaring the certain connexion between faith and salvation, which makes nothing against the doctrine of particular redemption! Christ said, that the Holy Ghost should, when he came, 'reprove the world of sin, because they believed not on him'; but the world he was to convince cannot be understood of all men, or every individual man, seeing millions were dead long before that time. The apostle declared, that 'God now commands all men every where to repent'; but the words imply that he did not always do it; 'The times of ignorance God winked at': But now, by diffusing the light of his word among the heathen world, he more generally called men off from their idolatries, to the knowledge and worship of the true God. Every individual man in the world cannot therefore be comprehended in the apostle's expressions. If we suppose all men, strictly speaking, were called to believe, we must enquire what it is that they are called to believe: To say it is that Christ died for them, is to take for granted the thing in question, whether he died for all men: To believe that Christ is the true and only Saviour, and to receive him, and depend upon him for salvation, as revealed in the gospel, is that faith which men are called to by the preaching of the gospel, and which has the promise of eternal life annexed to it; but this does not necessarily suppose that Christ died for all men.

There is a sufficient ground to preach the gospel to all, and for any person, who hears it, to hearken to the call of the gospel, seeing there are many that shall be saved. It would be thought not unreasonable to urge all husbandmen to plough and sow their lands, or all merchants to send their effects abroad, because all of the one sort shall not have good crops, nor will all of the other sort have good returns: It is sufficient to put them upon action, that some, nay, many have. Ministers are compared to sowers, Matt. 13:3, and they, as well as husbandmen, are in 'the morning to sow their seed, and in the evening not to withhold their hand, not knowing whether shall prosper, this or that', Eccles. 11:6. There are three things which lay a sufficient foundation for ministers to call all their hearers to believe, and for any of them to hearken to the call: One thing is, *Christ's ability to save, to the uttermost, all who come to God by him*, Heb. 7:25. Another thing is,

God's command, 1 John 3:23, *that men believe in Christ*; this is *the work of God*, John 6:29, that which he requires, and that which he is pleased with: Besides these, there is the gracious declaration and assurance; 'That whosoever believes shall not perish; and that Christ will in no wise cast out him that comes to him', chapter 3:16; 6:37. Upon these grounds, the apostles pressed men to 'believe in Christ', and preached to them forgiveness of sins, Acts 13:38, through faith in his blood; for so God has 'set him forth to be a propitiation', Rom. 3:25.

The gospel declares Christ's ability to save all that come to him; that all shall be saved who do believe in him; that it is the command of God that men believe; and that such as do not, must perish. Here is warrant enough for ministers to preach Christ to all, and encourage all their hearers to believe on him. If they could truly tell men that Christ died for all men, yet they could not tell them that any more should be saved, than actually believe; and it is certain, that all who believe shall be saved. It is not my knowledge that Christ died for me, that is the ground of my believing in him; but the command of God requiring it, and the declaration, that whosoever does so, shall have eternal life. Upon this, I have not only a liberty and encouragement to believe, when the gospel is preached to me, but it is my duty so to do. In the Olympic games, 1 Cor. 9:24, 'there were many run, though but one received the prize'; but in the case before us, not barely one, but all who believe shall be saved: and therefore when the man put the question to Christ, 'Whether there are few that be saved?' he bid him 'strive to enter in at the strait gate, because many would seek to enter in, and not be able', Luke 13:23, 24.

The gospel is 'the power of God to salvation to every one that believes'; and seeing no man, who enjoys the gospel, can know that he is excluded, but by final impenitence and unbelief, all men to whom the gospel is preached, have the same outward call, and encouragements to believe, as all the saved have had. It was not personally made known to them beforehand, that God had chosen, or that Christ died for them in particular; but the general declarations and promises of the gospel were set before them; Christ's ability and willingness to save lost sinners, were represented to them; and the Holy Spirit enabling them to believe these things, and to embrace Christ, as he is declared in the gospel, the promise of the Redeemer, the salvation became theirs: And any person now treading in the steps of their faith, shall be a fellow-heir with them of the same happiness.

If these things be duly considered, it will appear, that there is sufficient ground to call all men to believe, and for every hearer of the gospel to seek faith, without the person's knowing beforehand that Christ died for him in particular. Nor can I see how the knowledge of that, if it could be had, by an unbeliever, would help him; seeing those who say Christ died for all, yet allow, that many, even of those to whom he is preached, perish; yea, many who have truly believed. And it is granted on all hands, that without true faith and repentance, there is no salvation. They who affirm that Christ died for all men, generally say, that he did not procure them faith, nor undertake that they should certainly exert their own natural power to believe, which they are supposed to have: Wherein then are they better than others, or so well as those who are waiting at the pool side, till the Spirit moves upon the waters of the sanctuary? which he will do, and make it not only possible, but certain, that some, yea, many, shall be saved; and everyone is to wait and hope, upon these reasons and grounds, that he stands as fair for salvation as others; and should be sensible, that whether Christ died for all, or only some, yet it is certain, that without faith he cannot be saved; that it is folly and wickedness to make his misery certain, because his happiness is to him at present uncertain; and, upon the whole, that 'It is good for a man both to hope, and quietly to wait for the salvation of the Lord', Lam. 3:26.

I might further answer to the objection, that the calling all who hear the gospel to believe, is the way to manifest the wickedness of men, and make it appear, that their destruction is of themselves, if they neglect or refuse this salvation; seeing whether Christ died for all, or for some only, yet they can no otherwise know that they have no part in it: Seeing it is very plain, and what all, who understand and preach the gospel, must, and do tell the people, that 'whosoever believes shall not perish, but have everlasting life'.

If it should be said, if all men who hear the gospel are bound to believe that they shall or may be saved by Christ;

then multitudes are bound to believe a lie, if Christ did not die for all men, seeing then all men cannot be saved by Christ. To this I would answer, that to believe that all men, who have faith in Christ, shall be saved, is no lie, but a plain certain truth; and it is as evidently false, that any man is bound to believe that he shall or can be saved without faith in Christ: Therefore, though Christ died for some only, no man who, under the gospel, is called to believe, is required to believe a lie; for all who do believe on Christ shall be saved. Besides, the first thing which a man under the gospel is called to believe, is not that he shall be saved by Christ, but that 'there is salvation in no other'; and that if he truly receives Christ by faith, he shall be saved, but not otherwise.

(2) It is pretended, 'that the doctrine of particular redemption *detracts* from the goodness and grace of God, and the merits of Christ; and therefore it cannot be true'. To this I answer, that the goodness and grace of God, and the merits of Christ, are more magnified and advantaged by the doctrine of particular redemption, than by the doctrine of universal redemption.

It does not honour the divine goodness and grace for God to leave all men open, not only to a possibility, but even a great probability of perishing, notwithstanding all that he has done to save them; and yet so it is, according to them who say, he gave Christ to die for all men, but only to render their salvation possible. That love and goodness which secures salvation to some, though a smaller number, must be greater than that love and goodness, which provides only a remote possibility for all. It seems to shew a great coldness and indifference, to leave it a second time to the mutable will of man, to secure his salvation, when man's will in its best condition, had ruined Adam, and all his posterity. Might it not well have been thought, that if infinite love and goodness was shewed to all men, as it gave Christ to die for them, so it should give the Holy Spirit to apply salvation to them, to make them willing to embrace it, and fix their adherence to it?

The scriptures, Titus 3:4, 5, set forth the kindness and love of God in 'the washing of regeneration, and the renewing of the Holy Ghost'. The apostle said, 'God who is rich in mercy, for the great love wherewith he loved us, has quickened us together with Christ', Eph. 2:4, 5. But how does this great love and mercy towards man appear, in giving Christ for all men, only to make it possible that they may be saved, and then leave the far greater part of them for ever ignorant of the way of salvation, and multitudes who do know it, yea, all of them, to perish in their sins, if they do not, of their own free wills, without any preventing grace,[1] procured by Christ, or secured to them by the Father, make sure of this salvation? Is this the way to exalt the grace of God, and the merits of Christ; not to procure a certainty, but only a remote possibility of salvation for men?

---

[1] That is, grace that precedes or 'goes before', that anticipates and supplies the need.—P.

If Christ died for all men, and yet leaves many of them, to aggravate their guilt, in rejecting such a Saviour, when it was known to God, before he gave Christ for them, what they would do, surely it would have been more favour to them, not to have given Christ to die for them, than after that, to leave them to sink deeper into misery, under the guilt of 'denying the Lord who bought them', as some affirm. It must surely torment the poor creatures abundantly the more, to think that when Christ had opened a door of salvation for them, no kind hand would be so merciful as to lay hold on them and draw them in.

Is it not an unworthy representation of the God of love, to say, that though he seemed to love all men, so as to send Christ to die for them, yet he loved them so little, as to leave them all to perish, if they would, notwithstanding? I may here argue as the apostle did in a lower case, when he said, 'Whoso hath this world's goods, and sees his brother have need, and shuts up his bowels of compassion from him, how dwells the love of God in him?' 1 John 3:17. In like manner I may say, if God shewed such infinite goodness and love to all men, in giving Christ to die for them, how was it, that when he saw their need of his Spirit and grace, and the means of grace, he should shut up his bowels of compassion from them, leave them to themselves, and never so much as send the gospel to thousands of them?

In a few words, it does not appear to discover more, or so much grace and goodness in God, to take a distant and remote step towards the salvation of all, in giving Christ to make it possible, as in giving Christ, grace, and glory, certainly to some, yea, to a number, that no man can number; and to say, that Christ died for all men, not to purchase grace and glory for them, but only to render their salvation possible, is to depreciate, not exalt the merits of Christ, for this is to say, that he so merited salvation, as that salvation is secured to no man; for what is only possible may never be. And if Christ by his death procured a possibility of salvation, he only removed the insuperable obstruction, that so man might become his own Saviour, which is to exalt the goodness and power of the creature, and not the merit and grace of Christ. On the other hand, that grace must be infinite which gave Christ to procure, and secure eternal life, for a vast multitude of poor perishing sinners. And that merit must be infinite, which not only paid their vast debt to justice, but also purchased for them an inconceivable and eternal weight of glory.

Thus, I think, it appears that the doctrine of particular redemption does not detract from the goodness and grace of God, or the merits of Christ, but that the charge falls justly and very heavy upon the contrary opinion.

(3) It is confidently objected, 'that it represents God as *partial*, if not *unjust*, towards his creatures, if when they were all in the same condition, he provided a remedy, a Redeemer and Saviour for some, and not for others: and the same may be said of Christ; for why should not all, in a like condition,

be alike dealt withal?' I answer, That if God may make no difference between his creatures, in the same condition, then he must either provide a Saviour for all sinful creatures, or for none; and then why was there no Saviour provided for devils as well as for men? Are they not God's creatures, yea, creatures of a more noble kind than man? Are they not sinful and miserable creatures, who needed a Saviour as well as man: Why then are they passed by? Why did not Christ take their nature, and die for them, as well as for mankind? And if there was no blame or partiality in redeeming men, and not devils, why should it be thought a reflection upon God, to send his Son to redeem some men and not others? Where many have a just and equal claim to any benefit, there the giving it to one, and withholding it from others of them, is unjust and dishonourable; but when none of them have any just claim to it, but all have deserved the contrary, there the case is far otherwise. Where many have deserved punishment, and some are exempted from it, without any satisfaction to the law, whilst others are made to suffer the law, there lies a charge of unjust partiality; but this is not the case before us: though God exempts that particular number from condemnation, for whom Christ died, yet it is upon satisfaction made by their surety and Saviour, and in punishing the rest he does them no wrong, for he inflicts upon them nothing but what is the proper desert, and the due wages of sin.

God in his word has vindicated this right of sovereignty to himself, to bestow his favours upon whom he will; as in this passage, 'Who art thou, O man, that repliest against God? Has not the potter power over the clay, of the same lump to make one vessel to honour and another to dishonour?' Rom. 9:20, 21. The objection of partiality proceeds from the pride and envy of man, as Christ informed us, when he said: 'Is it not lawful for me to do what I will with mine own? Is thine eye evil because I am good?' Matt. 20:15. We see in the daily distributions of providence a great inequality; some are rich, others poor; some healthy, others very sickly; some born deformed, others well shaped: some wonderfully preserved, others exposed to many perils; some have the clear light of the gospel, and millions know nothing of Christ; and, shall not God be just, because he is thus partial?

(4) It is objected, 'that the doctrine of particular redemption takes away all comfort from poor sinners; therefore it is not true'. To this I answer, that the word of God affords no comfort to sinners, whilst they remain in impenitency and unbelief. 'There is no peace, saith the Lord, to the wicked', Isa. 48:22. 'He that believeth not shall not see life, but the wrath of God abides upon him', John 3:36. 'Except ye repent ye shall all likewise perish', Luke 13:5. Supposing Christ did die for all men, yet that can yield no comfort to a man that lies under the wrath and curse of God.

Those who say, that Christ died for all men, do not say, that all men shall be saved, or that it is so much as probable that they should. They do not suppose that Christ is engaged, by any special love, or covenant, to save any man, who enjoys the gospel, any more than those who never enjoy it, or those who are in hell. Nor do they pretend to say, that all, or the greater part of such as enjoy the gospel, will believe and be saved; and if they do not, what comfort can it afford men to think, that Christ died for all men, when, if it is so, that will but aggravate their condemnation and misery, as rejecters of Christ and his salvation?

All who believe and repent have the greatest grounds of joy and comfort, though Christ died to redeem and save some men only: This is 'strong consolation for all the heirs of promise, who have fled for refuge, to lay hold on Christ the hope set before them'. But, what comfort can that doctrine afford, which leaves all men at uncertainties, whether ever they shall be saved, though Christ died for them, and they believe in him? Because by his death, as the friends of it say, he established no certainty of their perseverance and salvation, ratified no absolute promises, did not procure them persevering grace, or that guidance of the Holy Spirit, which shall end in eternal life.

How is the covenant ordered in all things and sure? What consolation can he draw from it, who, though he may plead the gracious promises of it today, may be excluded from all interest in them tomorrow, and have no promise to plead for his recovery, nor any reason to hope, that that blood, which he says was shed for him, shall do anything else, but plead against him, as one trampling it under foot? Whereas upon the foot of particular redemption there is room to expect, that where the gospel comes, some, it may be many, will be brought home to Christ by it; for *all that the Father hath given him shall come*; and if *they fall, they shall rise again*: The promises are sealed and sure; effectual grace and eternal glory are purchased for them: Christ loves their persons, and will not permit any of them to perish; he pleads his death for them, undertakes to protect and guide them by his Spirit, till he has brought them safe to glory. Though they see no worthiness in themselves, yet they may plead his special love to them, and his giving himself for them, not only to make their salvation possible, but certain; and thus he has given them everlasting consolation, and good hope through grace.

If we tell a man in distress and anguish of spirit, for his reigning impenitency and unbelief, that Christ died for him, seeing he died for all men, and therefore he may be of good comfort, how easily may he reply, Be it so, that Christ died for all men, and so for me; yet I may perish as well as Cain and Judas: If Christ made my salvation possible by his death, yet I may make my damnation certain by my unbelief. What will it profit me, that Christ died for me, if my own treacherous unbelieving heart shuts me out from salvation? I do not perceive, that he purchased either grace or glory for me; but I am left to my own free will, which I find set against divine things, and bent upon what is evil; I have no absolute promises to plead, no assurance that Christ procured the Holy Spirit to help such as I am, or that Christ loved any man living better than thousands, whom he left to perish in their sins; of what advantage then is it to tell me, that Christ died for me and all men? If Christ had been a propitiation for my unbelief, as well as my other sins, I might have entertained some hope, that I should have been delivered from it; but now, though Christ died for all men, I may perish in my unbelief, as inevitably as if he had died for no man.

This I take to be a just representation of the case; and surely it is not hard to infer from what has been said, that the doctrine of Christ dying for some men, to secure them grace and glory, affords more solid comfort than the pretence that he died alike for all, to render their salvation barely possible, but purchased for them by his death neither grace nor glory, but left them to shift for themselves, to get faith and preserve it, if they could, or else to perish, as millions have done before them.

Twelve Points of Application

1. If Christ has rendered the salvation of his people certain, he must needs be a *mighty* and *powerful Redeemer*. The scripture has assured us, that 'God laid help upon one who is mighty', Psa. 89:19, and the Most High is introduced speaking thus, Isa. 42:1, 4, 'Behold my servant, whom I uphold;—he shall not fail nor be discouraged.' It would be unbecoming the wisdom and faithfulness of God, to give the character of a Saviour to an insufficient person. Redemption is the glory of all his works, but it would have been the disgrace of them, if he had appointed a person to redeem us, who was unable to do it, and who had failed in the performance; for then the chosen seed had been lost, the design of his love had been disappointed, the Sun of righteousness had set in an everlasting cloud of darkness, and the wisdom and truth of God had suffered an eclipse. Seeing then God has chosen Christ to save men, and has proposed him as a sufficient Redeemer, we may conclude, he is such an one; for the infinitely wise and good God would never have made choice of one, who was not equal to an undertaking, upon which his honour and man's happiness so much depended.

We cannot doubt of Christ's ability to save, if we consider his person and qualifications. In his person he is God-man, *God manifested in the flesh*; all the perfections of God, and all the capacities of man meet in him. Hence he was capable of obedience and sufferings as man, and of bearing the weight of vengeance, as his divine power supported the human nature. As man he could be humbled, crucified, and buried; as God he could raise himself from the dead, fill all things, convert the elect, confound the wicked, triumph over Satan, and bring many sons to glory. The church is taught to place her confidence in this, that her Saviour is God; not a made God, but the Lord Jehovah: hence she could say, Isa. 12:2, 'I will trust and not be afraid; for the Lord Jehovah is become my strength, and my song.' If the eternal God cannot be a refuge, and if the everlasting arms cannot uphold us, who shall? where is salvation to be had, if not in him 'in whom dwells all the fulness of the Godhead bodily, and who has all power in heaven and earth'? When Christ's human nature was formed in the womb of the virgin, 'the power of the Highest overshadowed her', Luke 1:35, not only so as to produce that nature in an extraordinary manner, but also, so as that the Son was for ever closely united to it, from the first moment wherein the humanity did exist. Viewing the Redeemer in this light, we may well conclude that he is *mighty to save*. It is therefore very good advice which is given us, to 'trust in the Lord for ever', Isa. 26:4, 'for in the Lord Jehovah there is everlasting strength'. We may say of our Saviour, as Job once said, Job 42:2, 'I know that thou canst do every thing': he can do every thing consistent with the glory of God, and the counsels of his will.

Christ fulfilled the law, suffered its curse, proved his divine mission by miracles, and manifested his deity in his resurrection: 'he made an end of sin, and brought in an everlasting righteousness', enlightened many dark minds, bowed many stubborn wills, sanctified many impure minds, gave them first grace, and then glory. Christ even when he was suffering in weakness, seemed to yield to the malice of his enemies, and was dying under his Father's vengeance; yet to make it evident, that he was able to save, put forth an act of his almighty power, upon the heart of one who was dying with him, and first made him 'willing in the day of his power', and then carried him up to his celestial palace. 'This day', said he to the converted thief, 'shalt thou be with me in paradise', Luke 23:43. The consideration of the time, place, and circumstances of this conversion, tends much to illustrate Christ's saving power. Satan was now gaping upon the prey, just ready to devour the poor thief, who was dying in all his guilt and wickedness: one Evangelist tells us, 'That they that were crucified with Christ reviled him', Mark 15:32, though another says, 'that one of the malefactors railed on him, but the other rebuked him', Luke 23:39, 40. These two accounts may be thus reconciled: When the malefactors were first nailed to the cross, they both of them spit out the venom of their wicked hearts against Christ; but in a little time, one of them began to relent: he felt a divine power from the dying Jesus coming upon him, which opened his eyes, changed his heart, caused him to rebuke his fellow-sufferer, to pray to his dying Saviour, and to believe and own his sovereignty and kingdom; and that when both the Saviour and the saved were in the agonies of death: this was a wonderful instance and evidence of Christ's saving power. Whilst Christ was in this world, the winds and the seas obeyed him; his enemies fell at his feet, and licked the dust when he pleased; the devils fled before him; many believed in him, to the saving of their souls: all which makes it very plain and evident, that Christ was mighty to save, a sufficient Saviour.

Christ invites all the *weary* and *heavy laden* to come to him for rest; which shews his ability to save all such as come to God by him. Was there any guilt which a redeemed soul could contract, any power of sin in such an one, which Christ could not expiate and subdue, his invitation would be all delusion. It is necessarily implied, and supposed in the invitation, that Christ is able to save every soul that is enabled to comply with it. Christ's ability to save is abundantly declared in the scriptures: 'Is my hand', says Christ, 'shortened at all, that it cannot redeem; or have I no power to deliver?' Isa. 50:2; 'who will contend with me? let us stand together', verses 8, 9. There is no opposing the Redeemer; 'he takes away the captives of the mighty, and the prey of the terrible, for the Saviour is the mighty One of Jacob', Isa. 49:24-26. Satan the prince of this world is spoiled, judged, and cast out, Col. 2:15; John 16:11; 12:31. 'The handwriting that was against us, which was contrary to us', Col. 2:14; Gal. 3:13, 'is taken away, Christ hath nailed it to his cross: he redeemed his people from the curse of the law, being made a curse for them: he has abolished death, and swallowed it up in victory, and brought life and immortality to light', 1 Cor. 15:54; 2 Tim. 1:10; 'he is the life, the eternal life; his people reign in life by him'; hence *death* and *hell* are said to be *cast into the lake of fire*, Rev. 20:14. Christ saves all the redeemed from death and misery. The scriptures declare, 'that there is salvation in no other', Acts 4:12. 'He is God's salvation to the end of the earth', Isa. 49:6, which shews Christ to be a powerful Redeemer indeed. The promises are all yea and amen in Christ Jesus; they are all confirmed by him: the promised grace and glory are purchased, and shall be applied by him; and therefore he is a mighty Saviour.

It is easy to cite a great number of particular promises relating to the several parts of our salvation; but I shall content myself with one or two, wherein the Holy Ghost has summed up all the rest: 'This is the promise that he hath promised us, even eternal life: this is the record that God has given us, eternal life; and this life is in his Son', 1 John 2:25; 5:11. But in vain were such comprehensive promises made, if Christ was not able to fulfil and make them good. God has promised that 'Israel shall be saved in the Lord, with an everlasting salvation', Isa. 45:17. Christ then is not only able to repulse the enemy once for a little time, but to secure his redeemed for ever; so as 'the enemy shall no more exact upon him', Psa. 89:22, or pluck them out of his hand.

Christ's sufficiency for the work of redemption, appears from the *dignity* to which he is raised in the celestial world. There is a prevailing intercessor with God: some might be apt to think this to be an argument of weakness, but in scripture it is produced as a proof of Christ's ability to save: 'Wherefore he is able to save them to the uttermost, that come to God by him, seeing he ever lives in heaven, to make intercession for them', Heb. 7:25. Christ's intercession shews him to be an able Saviour; for the Father would never have admitted him to plead his merits in heaven, if he had not paid a full price of redemption on earth: his plea is not as a supplicant for mercy, but he pleads law and justice; and therefore says peremptorily, 'Father, *I will,* that those whom thou hast given me, should be with me, to behold my glory', John 17:24. He well knew that his sacrifice would support his claim; and his life in heaven is a glorious evidence of his saving power: so that every Christian may, with Job, rejoice in this, 'that his Redeemer liveth', Job 19:25. This shews that he has satisfied justice, conquered death, and is able to save us by his life: the same power by which he rose from the dead, and ascended up into glory, is sufficient to 'raise us up together with him, and make us sit together with him in the heavenly mansions, which he is gone to prepare for his people', John 14:2. Christ taught his people to build a certain expectation of their eternal life upon his, when he said, 'Because I live, you shall live also', John 14:19; he who is our advocate, perfectly understands every case, which he undertakes to plead: he is always heard, because he pleads a merit which is always acceptable to his Father; and he pleads for a happiness which is entirely agreeable to the Father's purpose and promise: they therefore cannot miss of salvation, who have such an advocate before the throne. He never intercedes in vain; God gives him his heart's desire, and withholds not the request of his lips: he prayed for Peter, that his *faith might not fail*, and the effect followed: he was recovered from his sad fall, and enabled to strengthen his brethren.—Thus the life of Jesus is made manifest in our mortal bodies; we are as dying, and yet behold we live, because Christ ever lives in heaven, to make intercession for us, and so is able to save us to the uttermost from all sin and misery, and that for ever. In the gospel-glass, we may see 'Jesus crowned with glory and honour', Heb. 2:9, which is a convincing evidence, that he has procured eternal salvation for us. It is not once to be thought that God would have given such honours to an imperfect insufficient Saviour: to what purpose should God have set him over the works of his hands, who was not able to govern and over-rule them all to his own ends? or why should the redeemed ascribe to him 'glory and honour', as redeeming them to God by his blood, Rev. 5:9; if he had failed in that work, and had not procured for them 'a crown of glory that fades not away'? Why was the gospel proclaimed, and the converting or comforting Spirit sent down from heaven? why were all the angels of God required to 'worship the Saviour, and minister to the heirs of salvation', if the Saviour was impotent, and the salvation of the redeemed either imperfect or uncertain? If Christ failed in the purchase, why was 'he exalted to give repentance and remission of sins' Acts 5:31? for surely, he that is able to do this, must be able to save to the uttermost.

In the great day, Christ will raise up all given him by the Father, without letting any be lost or wanting, John 6:39; Jude verse 24, saying to his Father, 'Here am I, and the children whom thou hast given me; a glorious church, having neither spot nor wrinkle, nor any such thing', Heb. 2:13; Eph. 5:27; this will be done with exceeding joy, both on the part of the Father who chose them, the Son who redeemed them, the Holy Spirit who sanctified them, ministers who espoused them to Christ, and on the part of the redeemed, who enjoy this glorious salvation. Christ's ability to save, will appear in the clearest light in that day, when 'he shall come to be glorified in the saints, and admired in all them that believe', 1 Thess. 1:10. If we believe the scripture account of these things, there will be no room to question Christ's power to save. Even such as make light of it now, the last day will reveal it, 'when Christ shall appear the second time, without sin unto salvation', Heb. 9:28, all sin being expelled out of the redeemed, and all sorrows removed from them, their bodies being the glorious mansions of more glorious souls, all the saints being joined to Christ, that infinitely more glorious head, good angels adoring the Saviour, and admiring the salvation, and evil angels and men lying under the feet of his vengeance, filled with shame, horror, and eternal confusion. Now, we see through a glass but darkly, but then the Saviour will appear in all the glory of his saving power.

2. Such as are redeemed, may with admiration think on an *all-sufficient* Redeemer, being appointed to undertake their cause; for herein regard was had to man's impotency and misery. God had tried the strength of man, when Adam was in the state of innocence the head of mankind, and the trustee of their felicity, he soon fell, and ruined himself and his posterity: therefore it was not fit to intrust our happiness in such a hand again, much less in the hand of a sinful creature. God saw it needful to appoint his own Son, to be our Saviour; he well knew his wisdom, power, faithfulness, and immutability, his love to his glory, and to the happiness of man: he laid him as a sure foundation, a tried corner-stone, able to bear the weight of the whole building. No less a person could either satisfy for sin, or turn a soul from it, raise a body from the grave, or conduct a soul to glory: 'no man can redeem his brother, or give to God a ransom for his soul', Psa. 49:7; nor was it in the power of the chosen seed to deliver themselves from the tyranny of Satan, or the miseries of the present state. Such a Saviour as Christ was therefore necessary for us: God suited the remedy to the disease; the strength of the Saviour to the weakness and misery of the sinner: *Such an high priest became us*, Heb. 7:26, was fit and

suitable for us; impotent and miserable sinners stood in need of a strong and merciful Saviour.

God would have his chosen, not barely redeemed from hell, and brought to heaven; but he would have it done in such a way, as should be most to his own and his Son's honour. The apostle speaks of *salvation in Christ*, with *eternal glory*, 2 Tim. 2:10, not barely *salvation*, but a *glorious salvation*: a salvation which shall be to the honour of him that contrived it, of him that purchased it, of him that applied it, and of them who enjoy it. Concerning our Saviour, it is said, 'his glory is great in thy salvation; honour and majesty hast thou laid upon him', Psa. 21:5. When Christ was going to suffer, he therefore put up such a prayer as this: 'Father, the hour is come; glorify thy Son, that thy Son also may glorify thee', John 17:1. God provided a mighty Saviour, who was able to retrieve the honour which the first Adam had lost; he came short of the glory of God, but Christ in all things acted to his own and his Father's glory, both before he died, and since. He was ushered into the world with the songs of angels, resounding, 'Glory to God in the highest', Luke 2:14, and he went out of the world into a state of heavenly glory, where the Father and Son are continually praised for this wonderful salvation: for which reason, among others, heaven may be spoken of as a state of eternal glory.

God resolved in saving men, to destroy sin, and to vanquish Satan. This was a work too great to have been accomplished by any other than one who is almighty. It required the wisdom and power of a God to make an end of sin, and destroy Satan; to turn him out of his throne, and to cast his infection out of the soul. Satan was strongly fortified, deeply entrenched in the heart of man; he was a vigilant and subtle ruler, and not easily expelled; he baffled Adam in his state of integrity, and gained the throne when he had no friends in the soul beforehand; how then should a fallen creature be able to turn him out, when a holy creature could not keep him out? how could human power destroy sin, when it could not prevent its entrance into the heart, and its infecting our whole nature? It was necessary therefore, that this work should be undertaken by one who was infinite in wisdom and power, and so able to accomplish it. Christ therefore comes forth, 'walking in the greatness of his strength, mighty to save', Isa. 63:1. God exercised his infinite love to his chosen, by committing the care of their salvation to Christ; he well knew all the designs of his love were secured by this. The kindness of God appeared in this, that the Saviour whom he appointed, was no weak one, but able to save to the uttermost: his power, grace, wisdom, and merit were all infinite; and therefore poor timorous Christians may safely commit their souls to him, in a way of reliance without being afraid. 'In his love, and in his pity God saved his people, and carried them all the days of old'; and thus he deals with them, at all times, and in the present time. We have a wonderful instance of God's love to his chosen, in his giving his only begotten Son for them. Salvation is not straitened in him; the divine love dilates itself in unmeasurable dimensions, in raising up for us such a horn of salvation as Christ is: the mighty God is the prince of peace. A Christian can be in no distress, which the mighty Saviour is not able to free him from. Every believer may say, in the highest sense, as Hezekiah did in a lower case, 'I had great bitterness, but thou hast, in love to my soul, delivered it from the pit of corruption, for thou hast cast all my sins behind thy back', Isa. 38:17. In Christ the mighty Saviour, all the kind intentions of divine love are accomplished, and therefore God from the beginning chose us in Christ, that we should be 'without blame before him, in love', Eph. 1:4.

3. How great is the *folly* and *misery* of all those, who seek to any other but Christ to save them! All the herd of idolaters 'fly to a refuge of lies, and pray to a God that cannot save them', Isa. 45:20. In what confusion will they be, who have neglected the mighty Saviour, and his great salvation, when God shall say to them, 'Where are your gods which you have made you? let them arise, if they can save you, in the time of your trouble', Jer. 2:28. Some say to the works of their own hands, that they are their gods; and no wonder, if when they have exalted a created thing into a god, they degrade God the Saviour into a creature: they see no need of an infinite fund of power or merit in a Saviour, who are so full in themselves; but to all the rout of Pagan, Romish, and Arian idolaters, those words of God may be applied, 'Behold all you that kindle a fire, that compass yourselves about with sparks, walk in the

light of your fire, and in the sparks that you have kindled; this shall you have at my hand; you shall lie down in sorrow', Isa. 50:11. They who slight the mighty Saviour, spoke of in the former part of the chapter, and set up gods and saviours of their own, will meet with eternal sorrow and anguish in the end, when they lie down in the grave, and make their bed in hell. How will it rend their hearts with a thousand agonies, when they shall be forced to say, 'The harvest is past, the summer is ended, and we are not saved', Jer. 8:19, 20, the reason of which is premised: 'they have provoked me to anger with their graven images, with strange vanities'. Is not this the case of such as set up a saviour, who is neither a god nor a creature, as well as of those who worship images, or trust to their own good works to save them?

4. How acceptable should the gospel be, both to them that preach it, and to them that hear it! Every minister who loves the glory of God, and the happiness of men, may be very glad that he has such a message to bring to the people as the angel had, when he said, 'Fear not, for behold I bring you good tidings of great joy, which shall be to all people; for to you is born this day a Saviour, which is Christ the Lord', Luke 2:10, 11. A mighty Saviour, an all-sufficient Saviour, who is able to deliver all who come to God by him, from sin and Satan, death and hell. 'How beautiful should the feet of those be that publish salvation, and say to Zion, thy God reigneth', Isa. 52:7. We have lived to see the message and the

messengers treated with contempt. What Paul says, 1 Tim. 1:15, is a *faithful saying*, and *worthy of all acceptation*, some think is not worth their hearing. A Saviour who pursues the designs of distinguishing unchangeable love, and effectually saves all the redeemed, is despised and rejected, but without reason, and at the peril of such as do it; for the 'despisers must wonder and perish; but the voice of rejoicing and salvation is in the tabernacles of the righteous; because the right hand of the Lord doth valiantly': when ministers are *clothed with salvation*, the *saints should shout aloud for joy*.

5. Has Christ rendered certain the salvation of his people; what *pleasure* and *delight* may they take in him! Whatever troubles they have in the world, Christ says to them, 'Be of good cheer, I have overcome the world', John 16:33. Have we strong enemies to fight against us? we have a stronger Saviour to fight for us; Satan and the world are conquered enemies, and the weakest believer shall come off 'more than a conqueror, through him that loved him', Rom. 8:37. Doth our heinous guilt cry strongly against us for condemnation? the Christian should comfort himself in this, that the word of Christ cries louder in the ears of God for pardon and forgiveness. A believer has abundant reason to rejoice in God his Saviour, not only because there is no other, but also because there is nothing wanting in him. In him there is wisdom for the weak, righteousness for the soul that is ashamed of its own nakedness, sanctification for the polluted, and redemption for

those who are waiting for the glorious liberty of the children of God. With what delight then may the believer sit under the shadow, and how sweet may the fruit of this mighty Saviour be unto him!

With what joy might we draw water out of the wells of salvation; what comfort might we receive from the mighty Saviour, could we but live upon him by faith! when the roaring lion utters his voice, when the world rages, when within are fears, and without are fightings, yet what rest and peace might we have in Christ, could we but know *whom we have believed*, and be 'persuaded that he is able to keep what we have committed to his trust, against the great day', 2 Tim. 1:12. Christ wants no power or will to secure the souls and the salvation of such as by faith commit themselves to him; he is *the consolation of Israel*, Luke 2:25, and the Holy Spirit is the *comforter* of the faithful: he takes of the things of Christ, and comforts the Christian with them.

When the poor Christian is ready to sink under the burden of the body of sin, he may take comfort in that deliverance from it, which he shall shortly receive from the hand of Christ: when the weak believer is dismayed with fears, lest the enemies of his salvation should overcome and ruin him; this may quiet him, that all the powers of darkness shall never be able to pluck one lamb out of Christ's bosom, nor the most feeble sheep out of his almighty hand, John 10:28.

When fear and horror shall seize all the Christless world, at Christ's second coming, the faithful shall lift up their heads with joy, because their mighty Redeemer then comes to complete their salvation. In the mean time, the Christian may take comfort in this, that though there are many changes and disappointments in the world, yet Christ is ever the same; and may say, blessed be God, for blessing me with all spiritual blessings in Christ, that in him the heirs of promise might have *strong consolation*. All things in this world will shortly fail us, or we must leave them; but here is the comfort to the Christian, that his Redeemer lives: though the heavens and earth shall perish, yet Christ is the same; the same in power, merit, wisdom, grace, and glory; and these shall have no end, no change. We have no reason to call in question the compassions of Christ's heart, or the power of his hands: That is a most comfortable promise concerning Christ, which is in Micah's prophecy: 'He shall stand and feed in the strength of the Lord, in the majesty of the name of the Lord his God: and they shall abide; for now shall he be great to the ends of the earth', Mic. 5:4. In Christ there is infinite everlasting strength to overcome all his people's enemies, to remove all their difficulties, and supply all their wants; the redeemed people therefore shall abide, the gates of hell shall not prevail against them; for their Saviour is great, and shall be so to the ends of the earth; he shall have a growing and a lasting kingdom.

Let us then, when dejections and fears prevail, fix our thoughts upon such scriptures as set forth the power and grace of Christ; of which this is one: 'The Lord thy God in the midst of thee is mighty; he will save, he will rejoice over thee with joy; he will rest in his love', Zeph. 3:17. If there be no loveliness in us, yet he will take satisfaction in shewing love to us, in saving his poor distressed people: his love is not confined within such narrow limits as ours, nor does he want wisdom or power to enable him to do whatever his love inclines him to do for our good.

6. What reason have believers to cast all their care upon Christ, depending upon his ability to save them! Every true Christian may say, if Christ's blood is not sufficient to cleanse away my guilt, or his wisdom and power great enough to chase away mine enemies, or his love strong enough to do both for me, then I am content to perish; but I know he can, and he will keep what I have committed to his trust: I have reason to trust him; our fathers did it, and they were delivered: I am directed to cast my burden upon him, and he has promised to sustain me; 'Trust in the Lord for ever', says the prophet, Isa. 26:4, and he gave good reason for it: 'for in the Lord Jehovah there is everlasting strength.'

In our passage through this world, to the heavenly Canaan, the church is represented 'as going up, leaning upon her beloved', Song of Sol. 8:5. Here is our rest, here is our safety; our strength consists in our dependence upon the strong and mighty Saviour; 'we are strong in the Lord, and in the power of his might'. Let us then make this use of Christ's strength, ability to save, even to trust in him, resigning ourselves to him, and depending upon him; to do in us, with us, and for us whatever may be for his glory and our salvation. Paul in his conflict fled to Christ, and found present help: he said to him, 'My grace is sufficient for thee, my strength is made perfect in weakness', 2 Cor. 12:9. The less strength the Christian has, the more Christ will exert his power.

7. How *inexcusable* will *unbelievers* be another day! Christ is a most suitable engaging object of faith: what is there in him to create a distrust? what is there not in him that may encourage a dependence? He has all the qualifications necessary to enable him to save his friends, and destroy their enemies, there is no want of wisdom, grace, merit, or power in him; he is most inviolably faithful in his engagements, and in all his declarations. There is, therefore, good reason to believe the scripture account of him, to rest and rely by faith upon him; and they who refuse to do it, where the gospel comes, will aggravate their condemnation thereby. It is true, they could not believe of themselves; but it is as true, that they of themselves put forth positive acts of distrust of Christ, think him to be false, and reckon salvation a fiction.

8. How *dear* and *precious* should Christ be to all Christians! He has done great things for us, he is doing great things for us, and he will yet do greater things for us. How should we endeavour to exalt him, to magnify him, both in life and death. The mighty Saviour can never be too highly esteemed,

or too highly extolled by us. God has said, he shall be exalted, and be very high: let us then grow in our esteem of him; *he is fairer than the sons of men*. The Saviour and his salvation will appear glorious when all the glory of the world will be turned into darkness and horror; and when Christ appears, the saints shall appear with him in glory: this thought should raise our affections, and inflame our love to Christ. Every redeemed soul should say, 'My soul magnifies the Lord, and my spirit rejoices in God my Saviour: he is my Lord, and I will exalt him; he is the chiefest of ten thousand, and altogether lovely': he fulfils the Father's decrees, glorifies all the divine perfections, destroys all God's implacable enemies, and brings all the chosen seed to glory; not one shall be wanting, nor the least spot or imperfection shall be found in any of them. How glorious is Christ in this appearance; the object of the Father's love, and therefore he deserves ours. Let us love the Lord then, let him be very dear to our souls, who is thus 'glorious in his apparel, walking in the greatness of his strength, mighty to save', Isa. 63:1.

9. We may learn what a *glorious church* the great Saviour will have, when all the saints are gathered together in one. The general assembly and church of the first-born will make no mean appearance in the great day. If three thousand were added to the church in one day, and multitudes soon after, what a vast congregation will all the saved make, when they meet together at Christ's right hand? It will then be seen, that

he did not labour in vain, and die for nought: the redeemed will appear to be a 'number, that no man can number, out of all tongues, kindreds, and nations'; which will be a full evidence, that our Redeemer has not left the salvation of his people uncertain.

10. What reason have all the redeemed to admire and honour *the sovereign saving grace* of God and Christ! Peter said thus to the Christians to whom he wrote, 'You are a chosen nation, a peculiar people, that you should shew forth his praise, who hath called you out of darkness into his marvellous light', 1 Pet. 2:9. A Christian may say: how is it, Lord, that thou shouldest love and redeem me, give thyself for me, and then reveal thyself to me, pour out thy blood upon the cross, and pour out thy Spirit into the heart of such a worthless worm as I? Lord, why did not I as well as others, receive the just wages of my sins? why did my Saviour pay my debt, when so many others, fallen angels and men, must be paying theirs for ever? O glorious, sovereign, distinguishing grace! not to me, not to me, but to thy name be all the glory: peculiar love calls for special thankfulness. I thank thee, O Father, Lord of heaven and earth, that whilst this salvation is hid from others, it is revealed to me; and that I have been enabled to receive the atonement, and to joy in thee through Jesus Christ my Lord. This is a thank-offering which becomes all the redeemed, but it will be done infinitely better, when the saints come to sing the song of the Lamb in the new

Jerusalem, according to this model of it: 'Thou art worthy, for thou wast slain, and hast redeemed us to God by thy blood, out of every kindred, tongue, people, and nation', Rev. 5:9. Those who stand with Christ upon 'mount Sion, having his Father's name written on their foreheads', Rev. 14:1, 5, who are redeemed from the earth, should often sing that song, which none but they can learn, 'who are the redeemed from among men, and are the first fruits to God, and to the Lamb'. But not only good works and good affections are to be given to their God and Saviour; but the redeemed peculiar people, ought to be zealous of good works. Those who are bought with such an invaluable price, as Christ's blood, ought to glorify him in their bodies and spirits: his love, as well as his authority and right, should 'constrain us, not to live to ourselves, but to him that died for us, and rose again'.

11. What *encouragement* is there for us to wait for salvation by Christ, to lie at his foot, and hope in his mercy! The saved are a numberless number, sinners of all ages, sizes, and circumstances: The Saviour set forth in the gospel, is able to *save to the uttermost, all who come to God by him*. Those who are left to their own wills perish; God works a work which they in no wise believe: they will not come to Christ that they may have life; but those committed to the care of Christ shall come; he makes them willing in the day of his power, by his word and Spirit, and the pastoral rod of his strength. It is good then to *wait at wisdom's gates*; for such as *find Christ, find life*.

There is encouragement to hope for mercy, if we wait for it, in the way which Christ has prescribed: He has said, 'Seek, and you shall find; search the scriptures, they testify of me; come to me all you that are weary, and I will give you rest.' The psalmist uses an argument which is grown much stronger since his time: 'Our fathers trusted in thee, and they were delivered', Psa. 22:4. We may say not only the patriarchs and prophets, but the apostles, the primitive church, and multitudes down to this present time, have trusted in Christ, and have been saved by him; therefore 'it is good for us to wait and hope for the salvation of the Lord'. It is our business to prove our election and redemption by our effectual calling. If we believe, we shall be saved; if we never do, then there is no salvation for us. It is a great encouragement that there is a Saviour, infinite in grace and merit, who will give the water of life freely, to every one that thirsts; and we have as fair an opportunity as thousands before us, who ventured their souls on Christ, and were kindly received by him.

12. Let us not *sink* under the *greatest discouragements* which we meet with in the course of providence. Valuable and useful instruments are taken away, or laid aside: faithful and able ministers die; but Christ lives still; and blessed be the rock of our salvation. Christ is *mighty to save* and with him is the *residue of the Spirit*: It is he that made those who are gone what they were; and he can give the same Spirit and gifts to others, or work the same effects, by less able and likely means.

We should then cry to the Lord God of Elijah, to pour out more of his Spirit on his ministers and people, that salvation work may be carried on, not by human might and power, but by the Spirit of the Lord. Christ has promised to be with his ministers and people to the *end of the world*, if they teach and do what he has commanded, Matt. 28:20. Let us then, in his own way, depend upon his promise, and wait for his blessing, who 'walks in the greatness of his strength, and is mighty to save; who gave himself for us, that he might redeem us from all iniquity, and purify us to himself a peculiar people, zealous of good works'.

> *Now to him that is able to keep us from falling, and to present us faultless before the presence of his glory, to our exceeding joy; to the only wise God, our Saviour Jesus Christ be glory and majesty, dominion and power, both now and for ever. Amen.*

*Some other titles
published by the Trust*

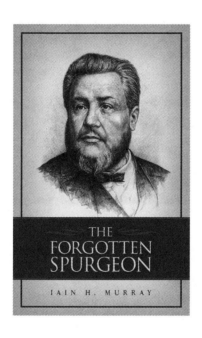

The Forgotten Spurgeon
Iain H. Murray
paperback, 284pp. ISBN: 978 1 84871 011 5

The Atonement: In Its Relations to the Covenant,
the Priesthood, the Intercession of our Lord
Hugh Martin
clothbound, 248pp. ISBN: 978 1 84871 291 1

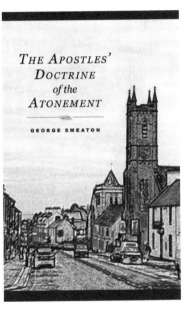

Christ's Doctrine of the Atonement
George Smeaton
clothbound, 520pp. ISBN: 978 0 85151 600 4

The Apostles' Doctrine of the Atonement
George Smeaton
clothbound, 568pp. ISBN: 978 0 85151 599 1

The Banner of Truth Trust originated in 1957 in London. The founders believed that much of the best literature of historic Christianity had been allowed to fall into oblivion and that, under God, its recovery could well lead not only to a strengthening of the church, but to true revival.

Inter-denominational in vision, this publishing work is now international, and our lists include a number of contemporary authors along with classics from the past. The translation of these books into many languages is encouraged.

A monthly magazine, *The Banner of Truth*, is also published. More information about this and all our publications can be found on our website or supplied by either of the offices below.

THE BANNER OF TRUTH TRUST

3 Murrayfield Road
Edinburgh, EH12 6EL
UK

PO Box 621, Carlisle
Pennsylvania 17013
USA

www.banneroftruth.org